W9-CFO-465

THE CUISINE OF
JACQUES MAXIMIN

THE CUISINE OF
JACQUES MAXIMIN

edited and adapted by Caroline Conran

SEVERN HOUSE PUBLISHERS

This title first published in Great Britain 1986 by
Severn House Publishers
4 Brook Street, London W1Y 1AA
by arrangement with Editions Robert Laffont, S.A., Paris.

This English translation and adaptation
© Appleround Ltd, 1986.

Colour photographs Daniel Czap

The Cuisine of Jacques Maximin was originally
published in France as "Couleurs, Parfums et Saveurs
de Ma Cuisine — les recettes originales de Jacques Maximin"
© Editions Robert Laffont, S.A., Paris 1984
[In the collection "Les recettes originales de … dirigeé par Claude Lebey."]

English translation by Caroline Conran and Caroline Hobhouse

British Library Cataloguing in Publication Data

Maximin, Jacques
The cuisine of Jacques Maximin.
1.   Cookery, French
I.   Title II. Conran, Caroline III. Couleurs,
parfums et saveurs de ma cuisine. *English*
641.5944   TX719

ISBN 0-7278-2062-1
ISBN 0-7278-2102-4 Pbk

Printed and bound in Great Britain by
Butler & Tanner Ltd, Frome and London.

Contents

Illustrations appear between pages 96-7 and 192-3

(Daniel Czap)

Preface

When I arrived in Nice I was a little frightened of such an emphatic style of cooking, with its unsettling aromas and enough garlic to make intimate conversation unbearable and seduction unlikely.

I loved the region before I loved its cooking. Then, seeking a culinary identity, I looked more closely at the vast reservoir of good produce this countryside offers, and I soon realised that it was that on which I must rely. I had to find out how to resuscitate, research, reform or simply rethink this cuisine right from its roots, to prove that the Niçois area was not just a gastronomic backwater, but truly the homeland of a culinary renaissance based on dishes other than the stereotyped pizzas and ratatouilles.

I had a lot to learn, and in finding out, some of the influences working on me were artistic, principally from my friends Arman and César, two outstanding and very different artists who helped me to find a new way of looking at presentation. The art of cooking is frequently linked to those of painting, music and poetry, but I personally believe that the closest affinity is to sculpture. Both arts are based on manual dexterity, on a sense of touch, on the ability to combine different elements in harmonious mixtures, and both use simple, fundamental materials to build the finished work of art. Sculpture, therefore, can be likened to the art of "cooking" with metal, wood and other materials, and the sculptor can respect the skill which his fellow-artist, the cook, brings to his profession and share his aspirations to extend the boundaries of his art. Arman and César, my dedicated friends, made their mark on their generation with their intelligence, wisdom, generosity and enthusiasm, not least in the field of cooking. I am grateful to them for letting me include some of their recipes in this book. César's influence can be seen in the Tian d'agneau, and the Tian de Saint-Jacques, both made up of compressed layers of different, but still clearly distinguishable, ingredients. Arman's influence shows itself in rather different ways. His talent for making many dishes from a single ingredient led, for instance, to a lobster menu in three courses, comprising a soup (made from the shells), a salad (containing the claws) and finally a fricassee made from the tail meat. In short, I would add to the traditional sources of inspiration to the cook the conversation of artists. Their ways of thinking and of seeing, can have a profound influence on the development of his cuisine.

JACQUES MAXIMIN

Introduction

Small, intense and wiry, Jacques Maximin, young chef of the celebrated Chantecler restaurant in the dizzily rococo, pink-domed Hotel Negresco in Nice, chose his metier at the tender age of fourteen. His work took him from the beautiful art-nouveau restaurant Chez Prunier in the rue Traktir to the more traditional cooking of the Pré Catelan in the Bois de Boulogne, and then, in 1972, to the south to work with Roger Vergé at the Moulin de Mougins, where he first began to enjoy the southern sunshine and the way of life.

Jacques Maximin, born and brought up in the Pas-de-Calais, about as far north as you can go and still remain French, was influenced then by a grey and green landscape and learned to cook with northern tastes; sole and turbot, leeks and potatoes, butter and cream. When he first moved to the Mediterranean he found the Provençal cooking hard to adapt to with its heightened flavours and extravagant use of garlic. But he soon found himself expanding under the influence of blue skies and the warmth of the sun, seduced by the beautiful produce piled high in the local markets – the purple and green artichokes, the salad plants, the "ratatouille" of vegetables which taste so much better in the south of France, the irridescent rock-fish, rascasse and red mullet, the lemons and the apricots. He took to making local dishes – pasta (Nice, at one time an Italian city, is passionate about pasta) aïoli and soupe au pistou. But as a northerner he also felt free to innovate and experiment. To begin with, he shocked many traditionally minded people, but also from the beginning, he had the support of influential critics.

Not all Maximin's dishes are Mediterranean in flavour, but much of his cooking does rely on the range and quality of local produce. Happily almost all the ingredients he uses in this book are now available from specialist shops, and increasingly from good supermarkets, outside France, and supplies are improving each year. Where ingredients may be genuinely difficult to find we have suggested alternatives. Otherwise, the recipes are substantially as Maître Maximin wrote them, with allowances made for the home cook, who obviously does not have the time and equipment available to the cooks in a large professional kitchen.

There are two kinds of recipe in this book: dishes for special occasions, lavish, extravagant and a triumph to serve at a party or a celebration, and everyday dishes which are straightforward enough for a simple dinner at home – the Caudière Berckoise, for example, a plain but exquisite fish soup from the north of France, or chicken roasted with walnut butter – for people who appreciate simple cooking. The cakes, desserts and mousses also range from the elaborate Kumquat Charlotte to the incredibly good water ices such as an exquisite Rosemary Sorbet.

Because olive oil is a vital ingredient in Maximin's cooking it is important to know exactly what to look for. He himself uses a very full-flavoured greenish cold-pressed extra-virgin olive oil from the Niçois region. A good first-pressing oil from Provence or a first-grade virgin oil from Tuscany will do almost as well. The taste of this oil, which can be a revelation to anyone who has only been accustomed to over-refined supermarket oils, is truly crucial to a dish like the Fillets of Sole "en Brandade", so you should make finding a reliable source of oil a priority before starting on the many delicious oil-based recipes in this book.

Garlic is of course also vital; try and find a plump purple-streaked variety from, or similar to those grown in, Provence and if it is not entirely fresh and has sprouted slightly, remove the bitter green parts from the centre of the cloves. When a whole clove of garlic is called for, you should use an unpeeled clove, crushed under a heavy knife blade so that it splits and can give off its juices.

Maître Maximin uses wild mushrooms (cèpes, girolles and morels) in many of his recipes. These can be bought, dried, at a price, but even a few, presoaked and added to ordinary mushrooms to make up the full quantity specified in the recipe, will give an authentic flavour. It is also possible to find the same or similar species growing in the wild, and more people every year are taking to the woods in summer and autumn to gather their own. This is not, however, a pastime for amateurs, as there are many toxic or indigestible species as well as delicious ones. You should not eat anything which you, or an experienced friend, cannot positively identify as edible.

Crème Fraîche is the cream commonly used in all good French cooking. It has a lighter, fresher taste than cream generally found outside France, and this flavour can make a considerable difference to the result in sauces where cream is reduced, as well as to desserts and pastries which use whipped cream. It can be found in specialist shops and large supermarkets, but it is also easy to make at home if you want to achieve an authentic flavour with Maître Maximin's cream-rich dishes. Add 1 tablespoon of buttermilk to each 500 ml (scant pint) of cream and heat to 24-39°C (75-85°F). This is below blood heat, and the cream will feel slightly cool when you dip a finger in it. Remove the cream from the stove and keep it, covered, in a warm place until it has thickened. This method works equally well for heavy/double cream and for whipping cream, which the French call crème fleurette.

The butter used in the recipes is always unsalted.

A number of the cold first courses and desserts in this book require gelatine. The author specifies leaf gelatine and this is certainly the best. It is now fairly easily obtainable outside France and must always be soaked, drained and dissolved in a hot liquid before use. If you cannot obtain leaf gelatine, powdered gelatine can be used instead, but it will not give so good a result. It does not need soaking. In both cases, do not boil liquid to which gelatine has been added and whisk vigorously when adding dissolved gelatine to a cool liquid or mixture to prevent lumps forming. One leaf of French gelatine is equivalent to 2 grams or 1 scant teaspoon of powdered gelatine.

You will notice that the author always specifies fresh herbs, which are available all the year round in Provence. Always use fresh rather than dried herbs; freshness is of the essence, even if it means substituting parsley for chervil or thyme for oregano.

Professional chefs cook in hotter kitchens than home cooks and with huge ovens which are heated to very high temperatures to supply the needs of many guests over a long serving period. Domestic ovens can never give such a solid blast of heat. We have allowed for this in adapting the recipes but it is nonetheless necessary to remember that your oven should be heated well in advance, and that roasting and baking utensils and the fat or liquid in them should be sizzling hot before they are placed in the oven. This applies specially to roasted meats and poultry and game. Always make sure the food is properly cooked through before you remove it from the oven. Chefs cook at high speed; a home cook with six rather than sixty plates to fill may find that food is none the worse for being cooked at a slightly lower temperature for a slightly longer time. This is where your skill and judgement will make all the difference.

In some of the dessert recipes the dish is cooked with the oven door slightly open, which may seem to defeat the object of the exercise. In fact, it is necessary to avoid the build-up of steam in the oven, and so you need to prop the door just slightly ajar, with a spoon. Many of the desserts use "Italian" meringue as a component part, a delicious confection in which hot syrup is poured onto beaten egg whites. For this, an electric hand-held (or preferably free-standing) beater is needed. You will also need a thermometer to check the temperature of the sugar until you are sufficiently confident to achieve the right result by timing. The technique is well worth mastering for itself, as quite apart from the recipes in this book it can be applied to ice creams and many other desserts. (See table on page 275.)

Maître Maximin is one of the foremost chefs of Europe and his admirers expect sophisticated and complex dishes from him, relying on the skills of his kitchen staff and the faultless quality of his produce to create the perfect result from each recipe every time. Some of the star recipes from the Chantecler are reproduced here, with hints and adaptations to make them accessible to the home cook. Others have been specifically included by the author for the home cook; apart from the excitement that comes from reading the world-famous recipes of a master-chef, the real pleasure for most of us will come from discovering a wonderful new way of cooking ratatouille or broccoli, a new recipe for pasta, a gratin of wild strawberries, or a recipe for salmon poached and served with coarse salt and an oil and tomato sauce.

When I talk to chefs and cooks outside France I always find that they are always most fascinated by the simplest ideas of the great French chefs whose chief fame lies in being complicated. When I come across recipes as simple and dazzling as some in this book, I can only agree with them.

CAROLINE CONRAN

APPETISERS AND SOUPS

Croûtes sèches à la moelle et aux champignons
Marrow Toasts with Mushrooms

Preparation time: 30 minutes

'wo
ple

6 slices from a French "baguette" loaf
6 thick slices of beef marrow
6 button mushrooms
a sliver of garlic
1 shallot, chopped
20 g (⅔ oz) butter
2 tablespoons walnut oil
lemon juice, coarse salt, freshly ground pepper

1. Toast the slices of bread until they are golden brown.

2. Clean the mushrooms and cut them in four pieces. Cook them for about 2 minutes in a small saucepan with the butter, garlic, shallot, walnut oil, lemon juice and seasoning and 1 tablespoon water. Transfer everything to a blender or food processor and blend to a purée. Pour into a glass bowl, and place in the freezer.

3. When the mixture is firm (but not frozen), spread it thickly on the pieces of toast.

4. Poach the slices of marrow for 10 minutes in salted water. Drain them, pat dry with paper towels and arrange one on each piece of toast. Sprinkle with coarse salt and season with pepper.

* A day-old brioche cut in rounds can also be used.

These toasts are delicious with game or a garlicky salad.

Editor's note The best way to toast the slices of French bread to a golden brown is to put them into a moderate oven for about 20 minutes, when they become an even pale golden colour all the way though.

" 'Rôties' pouvant accompagner un plat de gibier ou une salade à l'ail."

Oeufs de caille au plat
Quails' Eggs with Chicken Livers

Preparation time: 20 minutes

For two
people

20 g (⅔ oz) butter
1 firm glossy chicken liver
4 quails' eggs
a few drops of wine vinegar
salt, freshly ground pepper

1. Melt the butter in a small frying pan and sauté the chicken liver briefly, taking care that it remains rosy on the inside. Remove and slice very finely.

2. Fry the quails' eggs briefly in the same pan. The yolks must remain soft.

3. Remove the eggs and place on two small hot plates, arranging the slices of chicken liver round the edge.

4. Sprinkle with a few drops of wine vinegar and serve immediately.

* For garlic lovers, a small pinch of chopped garlic added to the cooking butter goes very well with these eggs.
* You can also serve the eggs on toasted slices of bread.

"Le resultat dependra du moelleux de leur cuisson."

Les croquettes d'amandes
Almond or Pine-nut croquettes

Preparation time: 1½ hours

For four people

100 g (3½ oz) fresh almonds or pine-nuts
30 g (1 oz) butter, softened
2 eggs
1 tablespoon chopped parsley
2 tablespoons flour
100 g (3½ oz) breadcrumbs
salt, freshly ground pepper

1. Grind the nuts in a food-processor. Add the butter, blend again, then add one of the eggs, the parsley and a pinch of salt and pepper.

2. Shape this mixture into little balls and put them on a tray in the freezer to firm up.

3. Roll them in flour, then in the other egg, beaten, and finally in the breadcrumbs.

4. Deep-fry at 350°F/180°C.

5. Drain, sprinkle with salt and arrange on a plate.

* You could also use slivered almonds

Editor's note The fresh almonds sold in Provençal markets still have their velvety pale-green outer coatings and the shells have not yet formed. When peeled, they have translucent, milky, slightly jellified flesh with a delicate flavour. Worth trying if you ever come across them.

"Excellent pour un buffet ou un cocktail."

Sardines crues au sel
Raw Sardines with Salt

Preparation time: 10 minutes plus 6 hours salting

For four people

12 very fresh sardines
250 g (8¾ oz) coarse salt
freshly ground pepper
3 tablespoons olive oil
juice of two medium lemons
4 slices of bread

1. Scale, and remove the heads from the sardines. Detach the fillets from the backbone and arrange them on an earthenware dish. Sprinkle with coarse salt and leave for six hours in the refrigerator.

2. Pat the sardine fillets dry with paper towels. Slice them finely into strips, sprinkle with olive oil and lemon juice and season with freshly ground pepper.

3. Just before you serve them, toast four slices of bread. Arrange the slices of marinated sardine on the bread and serve immediately.

* Have more coarse salt on the table
* Anchovies and small red mullet can be treated in the same way.

"Toutes les saveurs d'un retour de marché niçois."

Millefeuille de pique-nique
Picnic Millefeuille

Preparation time: 1 hour the previous day, 1 hour on the day

For ten people
12 very thin slices of cooked ham
12 very thin slices of Comté cheese
3 small fromages blancs or other low-fat white cheeses (20% fat content)
2 small bunches of chives, finely chopped
1 sliver (or slice) of garlic finely crushed
50 g (1¾ oz) toasted slivered almonds
salt, freshly ground pepper

THE PREVIOUS DAY

1. Arrange alternate slices of ham and cheese in a rectangular cake tin or terrine. Press firmly with weights and leave in the refrigerator overnight.

ON THE DAY

2. Mix the cheeses with the chopped chives. Add the garlic and season with salt and pepper.

3. Unmould the "pâté" on to a serving dish. Spread the cheese and chive mixture (2) over the top and sides with a spatula. Sprinkle with toasted almonds and keep it cool until you are ready to serve the "millefeuille". Serve it cut in delicate slices.

Editor's note The quality of this dish depends upon the quality of the ham and cheese with which it is made. Very good highly flavoured Comté is essential, and a classic unsmoked ham.

"De retour de Chine, cette 'Mignardise' m'a été servie à bord, je vous la communique."

Têtes de champignons aux cervelles, sauce vinaigre
Mushrooms Stuffed with Brains

Preparation time: 1 hour
Oven temperature: 400°F/200°C/Gas 6

For four
people

2 small lambs' brains
50 g (1¾ oz) butter
1 egg
12 large mushrooms, stalks removed
1 shallot, peeled and chopped
1 teaspoon Dijon mustard
1 teaspoon wine vinegar
salt, freshly ground pepper

Editor's note It is often necessary, if the brains have more than a few reddish veins, to soak them in cold water for 1½-2 hours before they are skinned and again after skinning, so that they become perfectly white.

"Une idée amusante qui peut même servir d'entrée."

1. Wash the brains in cold running water, skin them and remove the small veins and fibres. Blanch them by placing them in cold salted water, bringing to the boil and simmering for 14-20 minutes, until firm. Drain them and pat dry. When they have cooled cut them in small dice.

2. Preheat the oven. Melt all but a teaspoon of the butter in a small frying pan. Add the diced brains, season with salt and pepper. Sauté them over a low heat for a minute or two, remove and drain.

3. Beat the egg in a large bowl and add the cooked diced brains.

4. Clean the mushrooms, peeling them if the skin seems very tough, and fill each with a spoonful of the brain mixture. Arrange on an oiled baking sheet and bake in the oven for 10 minutes, or until the egg is set.

5. While the mushrooms are cooking, sweat the shallot in a teaspoon of butter. Add the mustard, vinegar and 1 teaspoon of water and season with salt and pepper. Stir, bring to the boil and strain through a fine sieve into a sauceboat.

6. Arrange the mushrooms on four small hot plates and pour a little sauce over each one.

* You can use calves' brains for this dish. They should be blanched for 25 minutes.
* Cèpes can be used instead of cultivated mushrooms (see page 8).

Crème de courges et sa "rouille" de pistils
Pumpkin Soup

Preparation time: 1 hour

For four to six people

500 g (1 lb 2 oz) orange pumpkin flesh
250 g (9 oz) courgette flowers, fully opened and very fresh
1 clove of garlic, peeled
1 egg yolk
150 ml (¼ pint) olive oil
100 g (3½ oz) butter
4-5 celery leaves (tops)
1 litre (1¾ pints) milk
10 medium slices of a French "baguette" loaf
salt, freshly ground pepper

1. Slice the pumpkin flesh finely.

2. Remove the pistil from each courgette flower, keeping the flowers to one side, and place in a small mortar or bowl. Pound them with the clove of garlic and an egg yolk, adding the olive oil drop by drop until you have a smooth thick "rouille", similar to a stiff mayonnaise.

3. In a large heavy bottomed saucepan, sweat the pumpkin in 100 g (3½ oz) butter with the courgette flowers. Add the celery leaves and moisten with the milk and an equal quantity of water. Season with salt and pepper. Bring to the boil and simmer for approximately 15 minutes. Blend to obtain a very smooth consistency, sieving if necessary to remove any fibres. Pour into a heated tureen and keep hot.

4. Toast the slices of bread and place on the table, together with the bowl of "rouille". Each guest should spread a few slices with the "rouille" and place them in their soup bowls and pour the hot pumpkin soup all over them.

* A food-processor can be used instead of a mortar.
* A small cooked potato pounded with the pistils will give a more substantial "rouille".

Editor's note A courgette flower has a very noticeable thick fleshy pistil, of an orange colour in the centre. It is easily removed by nipping it out with finger and thumb.

"Une crème de courges au lait additionnée d'une 'rouille' un peu spéciale à base de pistils de fleurs de courgettes."

Soupe froide de melon-pamplemousse au sauternes
Iced Melon and Grapefruit Soup with Sauternes

Preparation time: 20 minutes, 1 hour chilling

For four people

2 Cavaillon melons (Ogen or Charentais will do), fully ripened
2 small grapefruits
4 fresh mint leaves
¾ bottle Sauternes or other sweet white Bordeaux wine

1. Halve and seed the melons. Peel them and slice them finely.

2. Peel the grapefruit and remove all the bitter pith. Skin the segments with a small knife.

3. Arrange the melon slices in four plates, with the slices overlapping, as if you were making an apple flan. Arrange a rosette of grapefruit segments in the middle.

4. Pour over enough Sauternes to cover the fruit and place a mint leaf in the middle of each rosette.

5. Chill in the refrigerator for one hour, then serve.

* This soup can only be made when really good melons are available.
* If you have no Sauternes a Barsac will do very well.

"Plus facile que ça tu meurs!"

Crème de verts de radis
Radish-top Soup

Preparation time: 30 minutes

For four to six people

1 kg (2¼ lbs) green radish tops
1 potato, peeled and sliced
1 white onion, peeled and sliced
150 g (5¼ oz) butter
5 fresh mint leaves
salt, pepper

1. Wash the radish tops in plenty of cold water and blanch for five minutes in boiling salted water, as you would spinach. Refresh under cold water, drain thoroughly, pressing out excess water. Chop coarsely.

2. Sweat the potatoes and onion in 50 g (1¾ oz) of the butter for a few minutes and then add the radish tops. Add two litres (3½ pints) of water. Season with salt and pepper, bring to the boil and simmer gently for fifteen minutes. Purée in a food processor with 100 g (3½ oz) butter until you have a very smooth soup.

3. Taste for seasoning, reheat if necessary, and pour into a heated tureen. Throw in the shredded mint leaves at the last moment.

* If you enjoy radishes, don't throw away the tops. Store them in your freezer until you have enough to make this excellent soup.
* This soup is equally good eaten cold, with a little cream.

"Complètement délaissées, les fanes de radis constituent un potage de verdure absolument remarquable."

Crème de tomates vertes glacée et truffée
Cold Green Tomato Soup with Truffles

Preparation time: 1½ hours

For four to six people

1 kg (2¼ lb) green (unripe) tomatoes
250 ml (scant half pint) olive oil
1 white onion, peeled and chopped
2 shallots, peeled and chopped
1 green pepper, peeled, deseeded and chopped
2 artichoke hearts (from purple artichokes if possible) cut in quarters
1 litre (1¾ pints) still mineral water
500 ml (scant pint) whipping cream *or* thin crème fraîche
30 g (1 oz) fresh black truffle
salt, freshly ground pepper

1. Cut the tomatoes into quarters. Deseed but do not peel them.

2. Heat the oil in a large sauté pan. Add the onion, shallots, green pepper and artichoke hearts and sweat for a few minutes, stirring, before adding the quartered tomatoes. Season with salt and pepper, cover and cook over a low heat for one hour, stirring from time to time.

3. Purée the contents of the pan and mix the purée with the mineral water in a bowl. Strain through a fine sieve and chill in the refrigerator.

4. Just before serving, mix in the cream, which should also be cold. Taste for seasoning. Divide the soup between soup plates or bowls and float five slices of truffle – like water-lily leaves – in each. Serve immediately.

* This is an excellent summer soup; the truffles can be replaced with chopped fresh basil.
* This soup can be served hot.

Editor's note Mineral water is used in this recipe because the delicate flavour of the soup would be destroyed by any hint of chlorine in the water.

"Un mélange de couleur, d'odeurs et de saveurs."

Crème de laitue aux oeufs-ciboulette
Lettuce Soup with Eggs and Chives

Preparation time: 1½ hours

For four to six people

For the Lettuces
2 large lettuces
50 g (1¾ oz) butter
100 g (3½ oz) belly of pork, diced
1 white onion, peeled and chopped
2 litres (3½ pints) chicken consommé

For the Eggs
4 tablespoons white wine vinegar
4-6 eggs (one per person)
A bunch of chives, finely chopped
100 g (3½ oz) butter
salt, freshly ground pepper

PREPARING THE LETTUCES

1. Bring salted water to the boil in a large pan and blanch the lettuces for a minute or two. Refresh in cold water, drain and squeeze to extract excess moisture. Chop them roughly and sweat them in 50 g (1¾ oz) butter in a large heavy bottomed pan, together with the diced belly of pork and the chopped onions. Add the chicken stock, season with salt and pepper and cook over a gentle heat for 40 minutes.

POACHING THE EGGS

2. While the lettuce is cooking, prepare the eggs. Bring 1 litre (1¾ pints) water to the boil with 4 tablespoons white wine vinegar. Poach the eggs for 4-5 minutes apiece and plunge directly into cold water to stop the cooking process. Drain, and trim each egg to a nice round shape. Roll them in the chopped chives until they are well coated. Put on one side.

FINISHING AND SERVING THE SOUP

3. Purée the contents of the large pan (1) until it is smooth and velvety, strain through a fine sieve to extract the fibres from the pork. Reheat if necessary, stir in 100 g (3½ oz) butter, season with salt and pepper and pour into a heated tureen.

4. Place a chive-coated egg in each soup plate and ladle in the lettuce soup at the table.

* You can store all the outer leaves of lettuces in the freezer in order to make green lettuce purée or soup for the winter.
* Lettuce is one of the few salad vegetables which can be cooked successfully, endive is another possibility.

Soupe de lentilles aux pigeons et à la moelle
Lentil Soup with Pigeons and Marrow

Preparation time: 2 hours

For four people

For the Pigeon Stock
2 young pigeons (squabs)
2 carrots, scraped and finely chopped
3 shallots, peeled and finely chopped
150 g (5 oz) butter
500 ml (scant pint) dry white wine

For the Lentils
100 g (3½ oz) small green lentils
1 whole carrot, scraped
1 whole onion, peeled
2 cloves
2 cloves of garlic, peeled
1 stalk celery
1 sprig thyme
1 bayleaf
A few black peppercorns
30 g (1 oz) butter
1 shallot, very finely chopped
1 tablespoon chopped chives
4 thick slices of beef marrow
salt

THE PIGEON STOCK
1. Clean and singe the pigeons if it has not already been done. Remove the breasts and the thighs. Chop the carcasses roughly.

2. Brown the chopped carcasses in butter in a heavy sauté pan. Add the chopped carrots and shallots. Spoon off as much as possible of the butter when the vegetables are soft and add the white wine, and enough cold water to cover. Cook gently for 30 minutes to produce a stock. Strain through a fine sieve into a medium saucepan.

"Une soupe 'épicurienne'!"

26

THE LENTILS

3. Pick over the lentils and wash them in cold water. Add them to the stock together with the whole carrot, an onion stuck with two cloves, garlic, celery, a bouquet of herbs, peppercorns and a little salt. Cook gently for 30-40 minutes. Remove the vegetables and herbs and strain the lentils out of the cooking liquid, keeping both warm. Flavour the lentils with 30 g (1 oz) butter, a very finely chopped shallot and a tablespoon of chopped chives.

FINISHING AND SERVING

4. Sauté the pigeon breasts and thighs in a little butter. Do not overcook the breasts, they should still be pink inside.

5. Poach the slices of marrow for 10 minutes in boiling salted water and then drain them.

6. Slice the pigeon breasts very finely and arrange them in fans on four heated soup plates, covering half the bottom of each plate. Pile the lentils in the other half of each plate and place a slice of poached marrow together with a pigeon thigh in the middle. Serve to your guests.

7. Season the lentil broth with salt and pepper and add a nut of butter. Serve very hot in a heated tureen. Your guests will appreciate this method of serving because it allows them to enjoy the soup at the same time as the ingredients from which it is made.

* You can also use an old partridge for this dish instead of pigeons, cooking it for the same length of time as the lentils, but the result will not be as juicy as the pink fillets from the pigeon breasts.

Crème d'oignons doux caramélisés
Caramelised Onion Soup

Preparation time: 1½ hours

For four to six people
1 kg (2¼ lbs) white onions
100 g (3½ oz) butter
2 tablespoons caster sugar
1 tablespoon red wine vinegar
250 ml (scant half pint) dry port
6 egg yolks
6 tablespoons crème fraîche (double cream)
salt, white pepper, Cayenne pepper
toasted slices of French bread
grated cheese (Comté, Emmenthal etc.)

"L'âcreté de l'oignon est compensée par une liaison porto-crème."

MAKING THE SOUP

1. Skin the onions and chop them finely. Melt the butter in a large heavy-bottomed pan, add the onions and cook until they have turned golden brown. Stir constantly to ensure they do not catch and burn. When they have softened into a near-purée, after about half an hour, add 2 litres (3½ pints) water and season with salt and pepper. Bring to the boil and simmer for 30 minutes over a low heat. Strain into a bowl pressing the onions down with the back of a wooden spoon to extract all the juices, and keep warm.

FINISHING AND SERVING THE SOUP

2. Melt the sugar in a small saucepan until it is a light golden caramel. Away from the heat, pour in the vinegar and then the port. Mix well, bring to the boil, dissolve the caramel, and strain into a bowl. Set aside in a warm place.

3. Whisk the egg yolks and cream together in a large bowl. Pour in the hot caramel mixture (2), mix thoroughly and then beat in the soup (1). Transfer the mixture to a large saucepan and heat gently, stirring constantly with a wooden spoon until the soup becomes creamy. If necessary, use a food processor or hand-held electric beater to obtain a really smooth creamy soup. Taste and correct seasoning, including a dash of Cayenne pepper.

4. Serve immediately, accompanied by toasted slices of bread and a bowl of grated cheese.

* You need only the juices of the onions for this soup.
* You can spread the leftover onion "jam" on the toasted bread.

Consommé de volaille rose
Pink Chicken Consommé

Preparation time: 2½ hours

For four people

1 chicken, free-range if possible, plucked and cleaned
1 small cooked beetroot, 100 g (3½ oz) whole and with its skin on
2 stalks of celery
2 carrots
1 leek
1 onion, cut in half and browned on the cut side (*see note*).
1 sprig of thyme, a bayleaf
50 g (1¾ oz) vermicelli or other tiny pasta, broken into short lengths
salt, freshly ground pepper

1. Season the chicken inside and out and place it in an earthenware or enamelled cast-iron casserole with the clean and trimmed vegetables and the onion. Add cold water to cover, season with freshly ground pepper and simmer for 2 hours.

2. Remove the chicken, which should be almost falling apart, and set aside. Taste the broth for seasoning and strain through a fine cloth into a saucepan. Keep warm.

3. Peel the beetroot and cut it into fine strips. Divide these between four heated soup plates.

4. Bring the consommé to the boil, poach the pasta until it is tender and pour into a heated tureen. Pour the consommé over the beetroot sticks in the soup plates.

* Do not let the liquid boil during stage 1. If you do, it will go cloudy and require clarifying, which is always time-consuming and tricky for an inexperienced cook.
* You can use the chicken for a chicken salad with a cream dressing or as the basis of chicken croquettes.

Editor's note A good way of adding flavour and a little colour to a soup, broth or stew is to brown and caramelise the cut side of an onion, sprinkled with caster sugar, in a dry iron frying-pan or on a hot plate over a low heat for about 15 minutes, until it starts to smell good.

"Un bouillon de volaille couleur rubis."

Soupe froide de champignons garnie d'oeufs à la neige
Chilled Mushroom Soup

Preparation time: 1½ hours

For four
people
200 g (7 oz) button mushrooms
1 litre (1¾ pints) chicken stock
100 g (3½ oz) butter
juice of 1 lemon
4 egg whites
250 ml (scant ½ pint) thin crème fraîche *or* whipping cream
1 tablespoon chopped chives
40 g (1¼ oz) Sevruga caviar
salt, freshly ground pepper, Cayenne pepper

1. Clean and trim the mushrooms, quarter them and put in a heavy-bottomed pan with 1 litre (1¾ pints) chicken stock, the butter, the lemon juice and a little salt and pepper. Bring to the boil and cook briskly for 5 minutes. Pour the slightly cooled contents of the pan into a food processor and blend until you have a smooth purée. Pass through a fine sieve and chill.

2. Meanwhile, heat 4 litres (7 pints) of lightly salted water. Do not let it boil. It should reach 170°F/80°C and no higher.

3. Whisk the egg whites with a pinch of salt until they form stiff peaks. Using two wetted tablespoons, shape eight handsome quenelles, in a smooth egg shape, and poach them for 6-7 minutes. Remove carefully with a slotted spoon and drain on a cloth or kitchen paper.

4. Whip the cream until it is almost stiff. Fold it quickly into the chilled soup (1) and season with salt and pepper. Add a touch of Cayenne pepper and pour into 4 soup plates. Sprinkle with chopped chives.

5. Float 2 floating islands (3) in each plate and sprinkle each one with grains of caviar. Serve immediately.

"Des îlots blancs au milieu d'une mer de champignons."

Soupe de crustacés aux macaronis
Shellfish Soup with Pasta

Preparation time: 1½ hours

For six people

6½ tablespoons olive oil
2 leeks, trimmed and finely chopped
2 onions, skinned and finely chopped
4 tomatoes, quartered and seeded
6 small soft-shelled crabs (*see note*)
6 langoustines
6 freshwater crayfish
1 litre (1¾ pints) dry white wine
100 g (3½ oz) large tubular pasta
6½ tablespoons crème fleurette (whipping cream)
a pinch of paprika
salt, pepper

Editor's note You can use ordinary hard-shelled crabs instead of soft-shelled ones. Use 2 large crabs and return them to the soup with the shells of the other shellfish. Do not serve them as part of the garnish.

"Une simple cuisson de crustacés, bien parfumée, agrémentée de macaronis farcis!"

MAKING THE SOUP

1. Soften the chopped leeks and onions in olive oil in a heavy bottomed saucepan. Add the quartered tomatoes, the crabs, the langoustines, and the crayfish, and cook for a minute or two, stirring. Season with salt and pepper and add the white wine and enough water to cover. Bring to the boil and simmer for 30 minutes. After 10 minutes' simmering, remove the crabs, langoustines and crayfish with a slotted spoon. Reserve the crabs in a warm place. Remove and shell the tails of the langoustines and crayfish and set aside; return the heads and shells to the pan. At the end of the 30 minutes' simmering time, strain the cooking liquid through a fine cloth into a clean pan and keep warm.

PREPARING THE PASTA

2. Meanwhile, bring a pan of salted water to the boil and cook the tubular pasta until tender. Refresh under cold water and drain in a colander.

3. Bring the cream to the boil in a small pan with a pinch of paprika and simmer to reduce it until it coats the back of a spoon. Pour the reduced cream into a blender with the langoustine and crayfish tails and run the motor until you have a smooth purée. Using a forcing bag with a ⅛″ diameter nozzle, stuff each tubular pasta with the mixture.

SERVING THE SOUP

4. Divide the stuffed pasta among 6 heated soup plates and plant a crab in the middle of each plate.

5. Reheat the soup if necessary, and pour into a heated tureen. Ladle some into each soup plate in front of your guests.

Soupe à l'ail et brunoise niçoise
Niçoise Garlic and Vegetable Soup

Preparation time: 1½ hours

For four people

500 g (1 lb 2 oz) garlic
1 each of the following: courgette, aubergine, red pepper, green pepper, onion, all cleaned and trimmed, and cut into very small dice
1 tomato, skinned, deseeded and diced
6½ tablespoons olive oil
1 sprig of basil
4 eggs
1 teaspoon chopped chives
50 g (2 oz) butter
salt, freshly ground pepper

"Une soupe vieille comme le monde!"

1. Peel the cloves of garlic and put them in a pan containing 2 litres (3½ pints) cold water. Salt lightly and bring to the boil. Simmer very gently for 1 hour.

2. Meanwhile, cook each vegetable (except the tomato) separately in a little olive oil until tender. Drain and put together in a bowl.

3. Chop the basil and add to the "melted" vegetables. Add the diced tomato and mix gently. Divide the vegetables between 4 soup plates.

4. When the garlic is cooked, take off the heat and allow to rest for a few minutes. Then strain the cooking liquid into another saucepan and keep it hot. Mash the cooked garlic with a fork.

MAKING THE GARLIC OMELETTE
5. Break the eggs into a bowl, add the garlic purée, season with salt and pepper and beat thoroughly. Add a few chopped chives and make four small omelettes in the usual way, rolling them up neatly. Let them cool slightly and slice them crosswise. Arrange these little rolls over the cooked vegetables in their soup plates (3).

FINISHING AND SERVING THE SOUP
6. Reheat the soup (4) if necessary and serve in a heated tureen. Ladle the soup over the vegetables and omelette rolls in each plate at the table.

* If you want to create a pretty effect, arrange the vegetables in tiny bouquets according to variety, alternating the colours, and make a coronet of omelette rounds in the middle.

Pistou Marin
Seafood Pistou

Preparation time: 1 hour

For six people

For the Soup
1 each of the following: carrot, courgette, small turnip, leek, celery
    stalk with its leaves, all washed, trimmed and cut into small dice
50 g (1¾ oz) French beans, cut in 1 inch lengths
30 mussels
6 langoustines (Dublin Bay Prawns)
1 fillet weighing about 100 g (3½ oz) of each of the following:
    sole, rascasse and John Dory (Saint Pierre)
100 g (3½ oz) small macaroni
100 g (3½ oz) freshly grated Parmesan cheese
salt, freshly ground pepper

For the Pistou
2 ripe tomatoes, skinned, halved and deseeded
6 cloves of garlic, peeled
6 basil leaves
250 ml (scant half pint) olive oil

Editor's note A food processor can be used to make the pistou, but is inclined to give a more emulsified and less authentic result.

"Soupe de légumes et soupe de poissons, le tout à la fois."

PREPARING THE SOUP

1. Put all the vegetables except the beans and the tomatoes into a large pot containing 4 litres (7 pints) cold salted water. Bring to the boil and simmer until the vegetables are cooked. Set aside.

2. Scrape and wash the mussels under cold running water and place them in a large covered pan with a very little water over a medium heat until they open. Discard any which are already open when you clean them and any which do not open over the heat. Keep the cooking liquid, add a little more water, bring to simmering point and poach the langoustines for 10 minutes. Meanwhile, remove the mussels from their shells. When the langoustines are cooked, remove them and shell the tails.

3. Slice the fillets of fish finely, into small escalopes ⅛" thick, and divide them between six soup plates, making sure each person gets some of each kind of fish. Add the mussels and langoustine tails, season with salt and pepper and put aside in a warm place, unless you are preparing this part of the dish in advance, in which case store in the refrigerator until needed.

MAKING THE PISTOU

4. Grill the tomatoes, chop them finely. Pound the garlic with the basil leaves, until they are a pureé and then add the chopped grilled tomatoes. Pound again, adding the olive oil drop by drop, and transfer the "Pistou" to a sauceboat or bowl.

FINISHING AND SERVING THE SOUP

5. Cook the pasta in the soup (1), add the French beans five minutes before the pasta is cooked. Pour the contents of the pan into a heated tureen.

6. Ladle the soup, which must be boiling hot, into the soup plates containing the fish and shellfish (3). The fish will cook almost instantly, and the guests can help themselves to the pistou and to a bowl of Parmesan handed separately.

* The slices of fish must be very fine indeed if they are to cook on contact with the hot soup.

Caudière Berckoise
Fish Stew from Berck

Preparation time: 2 hours

For four to six people

500 g (1 lb 2 oz) mussels
250 g (8¾ oz) cockles or small clams
400 g (14 oz) slices of conger eel, middle cut
2 small soles
1 plaice
1 dab
1 sprig parsley, 2 bay leaves
4 large potatoes, peeled and sliced
2 onions, peeled and quartered
1 leek, trimmed and sliced
coarse salt and black peppercorns

1. Scrape the mussels and cockles or clams and soak them in cold running water for one hour.

2. Meanwhile, clean, scale and wash the fish. Do not remove the bones. Cut the whole fishes in two and slice the conger eel.

3. Half fill a large pan with 2 litres (3½ pints) water to which you have added coarse salt, a few peppercorns, the parsley and bayleaves tied with a thread, the onions, potatoes and leeks. Simmer over a low heat for 15 minutes, then add the slices of conger eel. Five minutes later, add the other fish followed by the mussels and cockles, still in their shells.

4. When the shellfish have opened, the caudière is ready to eat, either as it is, or with the cooking liquid served separately in soup bowls.

* At a time when nearly all fish is filleted, for convenience of serving and eating, it is a great pleasure to rediscover the flavour of fish cooked on the bone.

Editor's note This is an extremely pure and clean-tasting dish in which you can taste the fine flavours of the different fish and shellfish in shells.

The "Caudière"

"Caudière" is the name given in the coastal areas of the Pas-de-Calais (Etaples, Le Touquet, Berck) to a grand dish of white fish, potatotes and mussels cooked in a big cooking pot or cauldron, to which everyone helps themselves, according to their tastes. The small port of Berck, on the Côte d'Opale, still had, well into the nineteen-sixties, its little fleet of fishing boats called "Berckois". These wooden boats still bore sails at the turn of the century but have since been gradually converted to diesel engines. Solidly built, they actually ran aground at low tide and were used only for inshore fishing at night. A far cry from the fleets of modern trawlers, they represented a kind of seamanship that has since disappeared. When the fleet came in at dawn the people of Berck and its surrounding countryside were waiting for them, with great excitement, hardly allowing the crews to change into dry clothes after a wet night at sea, as they clamoured to get their hands on the catch, often without stopping to weigh it. Soles, whiting, plaice, dabs, mackerel and other fish would all appear, cooked any old way on the tables of the town. For it is a fact that the region, though rich in good ingredients, cannot be called gastronomic in the true sense of the word. I will always remember my mother calling out to my father, when we had the bistro at Rang-du-Fliers and he was going to fetch ice from the bar, "Georges, bring us back a good caudière". Here is the recipe, simple, rough and countrified, like the people who make it. Isn't that, in actual fact, proper cooking?

Thé chaud de légumes au pistou glacé
Hot Vegetable Tea with Iced Pistou

Preparation time: 1 hour, plus the time taken to prepare the
vegetables the previous evening

For four to
six people
on two or
three
occasions

1 kg (2¼ lb) each of the following: carrots, celeriac, turnips, leeks
100 g (3½ oz) peeled cloves of garlic
500 ml (scant pint) finest quality olive oil
10 leaves of basil
celery salt, freshly ground pepper

Editor's note 225°F/110°C/Gas ¼ is about the right temperature; the simmering oven of an Aga would be ideal.

"Des poudres odorantes et de l'huile glacée."

THE NIGHT BEFORE

1. Wash, trim and dry all the vegetables. Grate the carrots, celeriac and turnips finely, keeping each variety separate. Chop the leeks very finely.

2. Spread the vegetables out (still keeping them separate from each other) on a cloth or kitchen paper on a baking sheet or sheets. Put to dry overnight in a *very* low oven.

THE NEXT DAY

3. Make sure the vegetables are all quite dry. Pound each variety to a powder separately, either in a mortar or in a food-processor. Store the powders in airtight tins in a cool dry place. They are now ready to use as you wish, at times, and in combinations, which take your fancy. To use them, place approximately 50 g (1¾ oz) of powder in a little square of fine muslin and secure with a thread. The result will be rather like a teabag.

MAKING THE ICED PISTOU

Cook the peeled cloves of garlic in boiling salted water for 15 minutes. Drain and purée. Add the olive oil and the fresh basil, finely chopped. Mix and pour into an electric ice cream maker or sorbetière. The pistou will thicken and lighten in colour. When it is the consistency of ice cream, spoon it into a container suitable for the freezer. Using a melon-baller, scoop out enough little balls of frozen pistou to fill a small bowl. Keep in the freezer until needed.

MAKING THE TEA

Bring 2 litres (3½ pints) of water, to which you have added celery salt and pepper, to the boil. Pour over four little vegetable sachets, cover and allow to infuse 5-10 minutes, according to your taste. When the tea is sufficiently strong and fragrant remove and discard the sachets. Pour the hot tea into a heated tureen and ladle into four to six heated soup plates. Pass the bowl of frozen pistou balls so that the guests may help themselves according to taste. The pistou will melt slowly in the hot soup, the flavour suffusing the whole plateful.

* If you do not have a sorbetière, you can freeze your pistou in small containers, but it isn't the same thing, of course.

Soupe d'écrevisses à la coriandre
Crayfish Soup with Coriander

Preparation time: 45 minutes

For four
people

48 live freshwater crayfish *or* Dublin Bay Prawns
6½ tablespoons olive oil
500 ml (scant pint) dry white wine
3-4 sprigs fresh green coriander
100 g (3½ oz) butter
salt, freshly ground pepper

1. Remove the central fin of each crayfish and thus remove the small black thread which is the creature's intestine.

2. Heat the oil in a large sauté pan and when it is very hot throw in the crayfish and stir them briskly. When they have all turned red, drain them in a colander while you pour off the cooking oil, then return them to the pan. Add the wine and enough water to cover all the crayfish. Bring to the boil, cook for five minutes and then remove the crayfish. Separate the tails from the heads. Pound the heads and return to the cooking liquid. Simmer over a low heat for 20 minutes. Season with salt and pepper.

3. Meanwhile, shell the crayfish tails and arrange them in four soup plates. Sprinkle with leaves of coriander and set aside.

4. Strain the soup (2) through a very fine sieve or a cloth to remove all debris and impurities. The soup must be as clear as possible. Reheat, season with salt and pepper, add 100 g (3½ oz) butter in small dice. Swirl the pan until the butter is amalgamated with the soup, and serve in a heated tureen. In front of your guests, ladle the hot soup over the crayfish and coriander in the soup plates (3).

* This soup can be made with small langoustines, but I must tell you that freshwater crayfish, especially the variety known as "écrevisses pattes rouges" are, though difficult to obtain, vastly superior in flavour.
* If you cannot find fresh coriander (easy to grow and readily available in Middle Eastern and Oriental supermarkets) you can use a teaspoon of crushed coriander seeds.

"Une soupe d'écrevisses au goût d'écrevisses."

FIRST COURSES AND SALADS

Terrine charcutière aux trois langues
Three-tongue Terrine

Preparation time: 4 hours, plus 4 hours to soak the tongues
beforehand, and 12 hours to chill and press the terrine

*For four to
six people*

For the Terrine
2 lambs' tongues (unsalted)
1 pig's tongue (unsalted)
½ a calf's tongue (unsalted)
50 g (1¾ oz) butter, 50 g (1¾ oz) lard
100 g (3½ oz) pickling onions, peeled
1 carrot, sliced into rounds
a bouquet garni
2 cloves of garlic, peeled
4 tomatoes, peeled, seeded and diced
white part of a large leek, finely chopped
1 litre (1¾ pints) dry white wine
salt, pepper, black peppercorns

For the garnish
10 cornichons (pickled gherkins)
2 hard-boiled eggs
a bunch of parsley
1 tablespoon capers

"Une 'hure' fondante de langues, rehaussée de condiments."

PREPARING THE TONGUES

1. Soak the tongues in cold running water (or several changes of cold water) to eliminate all the blood. This will take not less than four hours.

2. Put the tongues in cold salted water and bring to the boil slowly. When the water boils, refresh the tongues under cold water, drain in a colander and, with a sharp pointed knife, remove the skins and all fatty parts.

COOKING THE TONGUES AND THEIR VEGETABLES

3. Melt the butter and lard in a large sauté pan and put in the onions, carrots and tongues to brown. Add a bouquet garni, the garlic, diced tomato and chopped leek. When everything is lightly browned, remove with a slotted spoon and pour off excess fat.

4. Keeping the sauté pan on the heat, pour in the white wine. Bring to a slow steady simmer and add the tongues and their vegetables. Season with salt and sprinkle with a few black peppercorns, then cover tightly and simmer for approximately 2 hours on a low heat.

PREPARING THE GARNISH

5. Meanwhile, slice the cornichons finely into little rounds, chop the hard-boiled eggs and the parsley, and mix together in a large bowl.

ASSEMBLING THE TERRINE

6. When the tongues are cooked to a melting softness, remove them from the pan with a slotted spoon and cut them into small chunks. Incorporate them with the garnish ingredients (5), and stir in the capers.

7. Strain the cooking liquid from the pan through a fine sieve on to the mixture in the bowl. Mix carefully to coat everything thoroughly with the liquid, and transfer to a rectangular terrine. Place a board of the correct size on top of the mixture and press with weights totalling 2 kg (4 lb 6 oz). Leave to chill in the refrigerator overnight.

SERVING THE TERRINE

8. Next day, unmould the terrine just before it is to be served, cut in slices and serve with a sauce rémoulade and a salad.

* You can add a calf's foot to the braising pan (5). The result will be even better.

Salade de pâtes fraîches à l'huile de crustacés et aux palourdes
Pasta Salad with Crayfish Vinaigrette and Clams

Preparation time: 1¼ hours plus ½ hour to assemble the recipe

For four people

For the Crayfish Oil
1 kg (2½ lb) freshwater crayfish shells – from about 40 crayfish
1 clove garlic, peeled
sprigs of fresh thyme and tarragon
a bayleaf
500 ml (scant pint) best quality arachide (groundnut) oil

For the Salad
500 g (1 lb 2 oz) fresh tagliatelle (see page 189)
24 clams (palourdes)
1 tablespoon coarse ground mustard
1 tablespoon red wine vinegar
1 shallot, peeled and chopped
1 teaspoon chopped tarragon
2 tablespoons peeled, seeded and diced tomato
salt, freshly ground pepper

When you use crayfish, be careful not to throw away the shells. Dry them and use them for this fragrant oil.

1. Crush the dried shells in a food processor or mortar and half-fill a wide-mouthed preserving jar with them. Add the garlic and herbs and fill to the top of the jar with oil. Seal the jar hermetically and sterilise in the usual way for 1 hour. Put in a cool dark place to mature for a week.

MAKING AND SERVING THE SALAD

2. Strain the oil (1) so that it is ready for use.

3. Bring a pan of salted water to the boil and cook the pasta for 2-3 minutes. Drain and rinse under warm water.

4. Put the clams in a large pan with 500 ml (scant pint) water and place on a medium heat until they have all opened. Discard any that are already open and those which do not open when steamed. Shell the rest.

5. Mix the mustard and vinegar in a bowl and add the chopped shallot and tarragon, then 4 tablespoons of the crayfish oil (2).

6. In a second bowl, put the drained cooked pasta and mix carefully with the diced raw tomato and the shelled clams and add the crayfish vinaigrette (5). Taste for seasoning and add salt and pepper if necessary. Serve the salad tepid, on individual plates.

* You can save time by buying ready-made fresh pasta.
* Add a spoonful of oil to the cooking water for the pasta: it will prevent them from sticking.
* The crayfish oil, once sterilised, will keep for up to a year in the refrigerator, and can be used to dress other salads.

Soufflé glacé aux artichauts violets
Iced Artichoke Soufflés

Preparation time: 1¾ hours plus at least 4 hours chilling time

For four people

8 large purple artichokes
1 tablespoon olive oil
250 ml (scant half pint) whipping cream
3 leaves of gelatine
100 g (3½ oz) foie gras (goose *or* duck) finely diced
200 g (7 oz) salad leaves, lambs lettuce or endives
5 tablespoons walnut oil
2 tablespoons sherry vinegar
1 tablespoon pale Dijon mustard
salt, freshly ground pepper

"Une entrée originale qui peut très bien figurer sur un buffet."

MAKING THE SOUFFLÉS

1. Place the artichokes in a pan of cold salted water, bring to the boil and cook for approximately 1 hour. Drain them and allow to cool.

2. Keep four whole artichokes on one side. Remove and discard the leaves and chokes of the remaining four, trim the hearts and reduce them to a purée with 1 tablespoon of olive oil. Season and transfer to a large bowl.

3. Take the four remaining artichokes and remove all but the outer ring of leaves, which you should trim to a maximum height of 1½" from the base with a pair of scissors. Remove the chokes carefully and trim the bases of the artichokes so that they will stand upright without support. You will now have four artichoke hearts, bare except for their stockades of outer leaves.

4. Melt the gelatine in a little warm water. Whip the cream until it is stiff. Gently whisk the gelatine into the warm artichoke mousse (2) and then fold in the whipped cream. Finally, fold in the foie gras, cut in tiny dice.

5. Fill each of the hollowed-out artichokes (3) with the mixture (4) and smooth the surface. Chill them in the refrigerator for at least four hours so that the mousses set firmly.

SERVING THE SOUFFLÉS

6. Remove the outer leaves from each chilled artichoke. Only their faint outlines will remain on the sides of the set mousses.

7. Make a carpet of salad leaves on four plates and place an artichoke on each. Serve with a sauceboat of vinaigrette made with 5 tablespoons walnut oil, 2 tablespoons of sherry vinegar, Dijon mustard, salt and pepper.

* The mousses can be chilled in little ramekins and turned out on to preserved artichoke hearts. Tinned artichoke hearts can be used instead of fresh ones.

For a note on gelatine, see Introduction.

Rillettes de canard "Trou Gascon"
Rillettes of Duck "Trou Gascon"

Preparation time: 3 hours plus 40 hours to prepare the duck and foie gras

For six people
1 thigh from a large fat duck (*or* 2 from an ordinary duck)
1 whole foie gras of duck weighing about 200 g (7 oz)
half a foreleg of salt pork (lightly salted), cut into pieces
40 g (1½ oz) shallots, peeled and chopped
5 tablespoons dry white wine
a pinch of nutmeg
1 clove
250 g (8¾ oz) strips of breast meat from a fat duck
bouquet garni
salt, freshly ground pepper, sugar

"Merveilleux cuisinier qu'est mon ami Alain Dutournier, en son 'Trou Gascon' à Paris. Un lien nous lie, celui d'avoir fait revivre une cuisine régionale, un peu personnalisée. Merci pour cette recette et pour la cuisine de l'amitié."

1. Sprinkle the duck thigh with coarse salt, a little sugar and a grinding of black pepper. Refrigerate for 36 hours.

2. Remove all the nerves and fibres from the foie gras, season in the same way as the duck thigh and leave overnight in the refrigerator. Soak the salt pork in cold water overnight.

MAKING THE RILLETTES
3. Put the shallots, wine, nutmeg and clove in a small pan and reduce until the wine has completely evaporated and the shallots are soft and just moist. Drain and trim the salt pork.

4. Wash the duck thigh (1). Remove the skin and any fatty parts and slice them into strips. Put them to melt in a wineglassful of water in a heavy-bottomed pan. Cut the meat from the thigh into large cubes and add to the pan together with the salt pork, the strips of duck breast, seasoned with salt and pepper, a bouquet garni, the clove and the shallots (3). Cover tightly and cook very, very slowly (80°C to 85°C/170°F to 180°F) for 2¾ hours, skimming from time to time.

5. Pat the foie gras dry and cut it into dice, adding it to the contents of the pan, which should by now be rich and unctuous. Cook for a further 15 minutes.

6. Remove the pan from the heat and, when the contents have cooled to tepid, remove the bones, the bouquet garni and the clove. Using two forks, shred the meats, mix them thoroughly and pack into a terrine. Refrigerate until you are nearly ready to serve the rillettes, which should be eaten at room temperature. They are best when allowed a few days to mature before being served with toasted pain de campagne.

Poularde en terrine pressée aux cèpes
Chicken Terrine with Wild Mushrooms

Preparation time: 3½ hours plus 12 hours refrigeration
Oven temperature: 275°F/140°C/Gas 1

For eight people
1 chicken weighing 1.8-2 kg (4-4½ lb)
100 g (3½ oz) shallots, peeled and finely chopped
250 ml (scant half pint) dry white wine
100 g (3½ oz) shelled pistachio nuts
1 kg (2¼ lbs) fresh or frozen wild mushrooms (cèpes)
250 ml (scant half pint) good quality arachide (ground-nut) oil
salt, freshly ground pepper

* The bones can be made into a reduced stock to produce a delicious accompanying jelly.
* This excellent terrine contains no eggs, no butter and in fact no binding agent at all. Its success depends on choosing the right size of terrine and positioning the weights correctly.

For a note on cèpes, see page 8.

1. Clean and singe the chicken if it has not already been done. Bone it out completely, taking care not to break the skin. (If you have not done this before, allow extra time to follow a step-by-step diagram in one of the many good books on kitchen techniques now available.) Remove any sinews and membranes you can see. Put the boned chicken on a plate large enough to spread it out. Season the inside with salt and pepper. Spread the chopped shallot over the interior, sprinkle with the white wine and allow to macerate for 2 hours.

2. Meanwhile, plunge the pistachio nuts first in boiling water and then in iced water. The skins can then be easily removed with a sharp knife or a fingernail.

3. Clean the cèpes and rinse them in cold running water to rid them of grit and dust. If using frozen cèpes make sure they are completely defrosted. Pat them dry. Cut them in chunks and cook them in very hot oil a few at a time for approximately 1 minute. Remove and drain.

4. Preheat the oven. Drain the chicken and pat it dry. Place it skin-side down in a terrine which would have fitted the unboned bird snugly, arranging the flaps of skin over the sides of the terrine. Pack the cavity with the mushroom (3) and the pistachios (2). Season with salt and pepper. Fold the flaps of skin over the stuffing so as to enclose it completely. Cover with a piece of foil and a lid and cook in the oven in a bain-marie, or a roasting pan containing an inch of water, for 2 hours.

5. Remove the lid and foil cover and allow the chicken to cool very slightly. Place a piece of wood or a plate of the correct size on top of the chicken and press with weights totalling 3 kg (6½ lb). When it has cooled completely, put it in the refrigerator for 12 hours or overnight.

6. Serve cut in thin slices, with a good green salad or a celeriac rémoulade.

Confit 'Palmyre' de lapin
Palmyre's Rabbit

Preparation time: 4½ hours
Oven temperature: 225°F/110°C/Gas ¼

For four
people

1 rabbit of 2 kg (4 lb 6 oz) – bred for the table
100 g (3½ oz) lard
200 g (7 oz) fresh belly of pork
10 cloves of garlic, peeled
20 little new onions, peeled
1 sprig thyme
1 sprig parsley
1 bayleaf
1 piece of pork rind large enough to cover the contents of your terrine
salt, freshly ground pepper

1. Cut the rabbit into large pieces leaving the bones in. Heat the lard in a heavy sauté pan and when it is very hot put in the pieces of rabbit and brown them lightly. Transfer them to a plate with a slotted spoon.

2. Cut the fresh belly of pork into pieces and brown it, together with the garlic and onions, in the hot lard. When they have browned transfer them to a plate with a slotted spoon.

3. Arrange the pieces of rabbit, the belly of pork, garlic and onions evenly in an earthenware terrine and add 500 ml (scant pint) of water. Add the herbs and season with salt and pepper. Cover with the pork rind and a lid.

4. Preheat the oven. Put the terrine in a bain-marie or a roasting pan containing 1″ of water and cook for 4 hours, adding boiling water to the pan from time to time as necessary. Remove the pork skin before serving.

* This rabbit can be served either hot or cold. If hot, serve it with fried sliced potatoes and if cold with a good salad with garlic and some "French fries".

"Chez moi, nous avions pour habitude de manger ce confit chaud; ma grand-mère 'Palmyre' en est à l'origine. Chaud ou froid comme celui-ci, le vrai goût du lapin cuit à l'os restera pour vous un merveilleux souvenir culinaire."

Mousse d'aubergines à tartiner
Aubergine Pâté

Preparation time: 45 minutes

For eight people

2 large aubergines
300 ml (½ pint) olive oil
6 fillets of anchovy packed in salt or in oil
1 generous branch of basil
2 cloves of garlic peeled and crushed
pepper (no salt)

1. Cut the aubergines into large chunks, leaving the skins on. Brown them lightly in a heavy-bottomed pan with 2 tablespoons of the oil. Add the anchovies, basil and garlic. Pour in just enough water to cover the aubergines. Put a layer of aluminium foil over the top of the pan and cover tightly with a lid. Stew gently until all the water has evaporated.

2. Pour the remaining oil into a food processor, add the aubergines from the pan (1) and blend until you have a very creamy smooth purée. Transfer to a chilled bowl over cracked ice so that it sets as quickly as possible.

3. You can use this mousse to accompany, for instance, a salad of artichoke hearts – simply add a spoonful to each plate – or as a spread for toasted rounds of bread.

* Those who do not like the skin of aubergines can grill them whole in the oven. The skin will come away easily, leaving only the flesh.

"Une façon comme une autre de remplacer le beurre. En tout cas, à Nice, on aime ça."

Pâte feuilletée de chou-fleur en gelée
Jellied Ham and Cauliflower Pie

Preparation time: 2½ hours (1½ hours can be in advance) plus 2 hours
    chilling
Oven temperatures: 1. 325°F/170°C/Gas 3, 2. 450°F/230°C/Gas 8

For four
people

1 cauliflower
150 g (5¼ oz) butter
200 g (7 oz) unsmoked cooked ham, diced
5 eggs
4 tablespoons crème fraîche (or double cream)
2 teaspoons fresh parsley, chopped
300 g (10½ oz) puff pastry dough
chicken aspic made with 20 g (⅔ oz) powder to 500 ml (scant pint)
    water
salt, freshly ground pepper

"*Une pâté en croûte avec de multiple variantes à adopter. Artichauts,*
courgettes, etc."

MAKING THE CAULIFLOWER FILLING

1. Wash the cauliflower, trimming away all the green leaves and separating the florets. Bring a pan of salted water to the boil while you do so and when it boils plunge in the florets for a few minutes. Refresh under cold water and drain them.

2. Melt 50 g (1¾ oz) of butter in a sauté pan and add the diced ham. Let it brown gently. Pour off the fat and add the drained cauliflower spreading the florets evenly over the bottom of the pan. Moisten with 500 ml (scant pint) of water and the remaining butter, cut in pieces. Cover with a piece of foil. Season with salt and pepper and simmer for about 45 minutes or until the liquid is reduced to a syrup.

3. Preheat the oven to the lower temperature. Take a non-stick loose-bottomed mould about 8″ in diameter and put in the cauliflower and ham with their syrup.

4. Beat 4 eggs in a bowl with the cream. Season lightly with salt and pepper, add the chopped parsley and pour the mixture over the cauliflower.

5. Place the mould in a bain-marie or a roasting pan containing 1″ of water and cook in the oven for approximately 1 hour. Remove and allow to become completely cold.

MAKING THE PASTRY CASE

6. Preheat the oven to hot. Roll out two circles of puff pastry, one larger than the other, 10″ and 12″ approximately. Put the smaller circle on a greased or non-stick baking tray and turn out the gâteaux of cauliflower onto the middle of it. Beat the fifth egg in a cup. Brush the edges of the circle with beaten egg and place the larger circle of pastry over the top. Seal the edges of the two circles firmly with your thumb. Trim any uneven edges with a sharp knife and decorate the top with a fork. Make a small circular hole in the centre to form a chimney. Brush the top with beaten egg and bake for 30 minutes.

7. Let the cooked pastry cool completely then pour in the cool aspic through the "chimney". Chill in the refrigerator.

SERVING THE PIE

8. When the jelly is completely set divide the pie into four and serve with a salad or a sauce verte.

* If your jelly is not sufficiently firm your pastry will be soggy.

Daube de lotte en gelée
Terrine of Monkfish

Preparation time: 2 hours plus 12 hours refrigeration

For four to six people

1 kg (2½ lb) fillets of monkfish
6½ tablespoons olive oil
4 carrots
4 turnips
15 small silver onions
10 firm white button mushrooms
100 g (3½ oz) butter
150 ml (¼ pint) ordinary claret
2 cloves of garlic, peeled and crushed
1 sprig of basil
2 leaves of gelatine
15 g (½ oz) each of chopped chervil, parsley and chives
salt, freshly ground pepper

"Un des rares poissons qui supportent très bien le vin rouge."

1. Take the fish fillets, wash and trim them and cut into medium sized dice. Season with salt and pepper. Heat the olive oil in a small pan; when it starts to smoke sear the pieces of fish for a few seconds on all sides, a few at a time, then remove them to a colander and allow them to drain.

2. Peel and trim the carrots and turnips and cut them into ¾" matchsticks. Skin the little onions. Wash the mushrooms briefly under the cold tap.

3. Melt the butter in a heavy-bottomed pan and let the vegetables (2) brown lightly for about ten minutes. When the carrots are just soft add the pieces of monkfish (1), the wine, the garlic and basil. Season with salt and pepper, cover and simmer for 15 minutes over a low heat. Put the gelatine leaves to soften in a little water.

4. Remove the ingredients from the pan with a slotted spoon and keep warm. Reduce the cooking liquid by half and add the gelatine lightly squeezed to remove the water. Stir well until it has thoroughly dissolved.

5. Remove the garlic and basil, stir in the fresh herbs and transfer the monkfish and vegetables to a terrine or individual moulds with the reduced cooking juices (4). Allow to cool and put to set in the refrigerator for 12 hours before serving.

SERVING THE TERRINE

6. Served either as a buffet dish or as a first course, this terrine goes well with a fresh tomato sauce, a sauce gribiche, tartare or other fresh-tasting sauce. Or, more simply, you can serve it with a salad of lettuce hearts with a cream dressing.

* It is essential to choose very tender young vegetables as the cooking time is so short.
* White wine can be used instead of red, and the cultivated mushrooms replaced with cèpes or chanterelles.

Aïoli de soles froid et salade de pommes de terres
Aïoli of Sole with Potato Salad

Preparation time: 2¾ hours plus 12 hours refrigeration
Oven temperature: 275°F/140°C/Gas 1

For six to eight people

For the Terrine
2 soles weighing 600 g (1 lb 5 oz) each
1 tablespoon butter
100 g (3½ oz) each of carrots, turnips and french beans
2 whole eggs
5 leaves of basil

For the Aïoli
10 cloves of garlic, peeled
2 egg yolks and 2 hard-boiled eggs
200 ml (⅓ pint) best quality olive oil

For the Potato Salad
4 medium potatoes
2 tablespoons crème fraîche (double cream)
1 shallot, peeled and finely chopped
juice of 1 lemon
salt, freshly ground pepper

A DAY IN ADVANCE: MAKING THE TERRINE
1. Remove the fillets from the backbone of the soles and skin them. Lay them out on a board, flatten them slightly and pat dry with kitchen paper. Butter the interior of a rectangular mould 12″ long, and line it with the fillets, letting the ends hang over the sides of the terrine. Season with salt and pepper and refrigerate.

2. Peel the carrots and turnips and trim the french beans. Cut all the vegetables in julienne strips 1¼″ long by ⅛″ thick.

3. Preheat the oven. Cook each vegetable separately in boiling salted water. Refresh under cold water and drain well. Break two whole eggs into a large bowl and mix with a fork. Add the cooked vegetables and the chopped basil leaves. Mix all together, season with salt and pepper and transfer to the terrine (1) on top of the layer of fish. Lift the ends of the fillets of sole and fold them over the top of the vegetables.

4. Cover the terrine and cook in a bain-marie, or a roasting pan containing 1″ of water, for 1¾ hours.

5. When the terrine is cooked, remove the lid and insert a piece of wood large enough to fit snugly inside the terrine, and press it with weights totalling 3 kg (6½ lb). Allow to cool completely and refrigerate under weights for a minimum of 12 hours.

ON THE DAY – MAKING THE AÏOLI
6. This is my own extra-light aïoli. Cook the 10 cloves of garlic in boiling salted water until soft. Drain them and crush to a purée. Put the purée in a bowl and add two raw egg yolks and two hard-boiled egg yolks. Beat with a whisk while adding olive oil in a thin trickle. Season with salt and pepper and keep in a cool place.

MAKING THE POTATO SALAD
8. Cook the potatoes in their skins in salted water, until easily pierced with a knife. As soon as they are cool enough, peel them and keep them hot.

9. Put the cream, lemon juice and chopped shallot in a bowl and season with salt and pepper. Mix well and then cut the warm potatoes in medium slices into the sauce. Mix very carefully to avoid breaking up the slices.

10. Unmould the sole terrine and, using a wetted, flexible knife, cut it in slices and serve either on individual plates or on a serving dish. Hand the aïoli and the potato salad separately.

* This aïoli can also be made with turbot, monkfish (lotte), gurnard (rougets grondins) and small cod.

Editor's note You can use chopped chives to flavour the potato salad and vary the vegetables in the terrine. Tiny cooked silver onions and small dice of barely cooked young courgettes would be suitable.

"Une autre manière, plus originale, que l'ancestral aïoli de morue, mais où tous les parfums traditionnels sont réunis."

Salade d'anchois frais et sa vinaigrette "à l'anchois"
Fresh Anchovy Salad with Anchovy Vinaigrette

Preparation time: 1½ hours

For four people 16 fresh anchovies
vegetable oil
2 red peppers
3 tablespoons olive oil
juice of 3 lemons
2 hard-boiled egg yolks
5 fillets of anchovy preserved in olive oil
4 leaves of basil
1 tablespoon wine vinegar
salt, freshly ground pepper

"Un travail de patience, récompensé par la beauté du plat dressé."

1. Heat a pan of vegetable oil until it is just starting to smoke and plunge in the peppers for approximately 2 minutes. Remove them and wipe off the oil. When they have cooled, remove the skins with the help of a sharp knife. Halve them, remove the seeds and the white fibrous parts, and cut each half neatly into seven vertical strips.

2. Spread out the fresh anchovies and carefully remove the backbones from the fillets with your fingers. Rinse them in cold water. Remove the dark interior skin of the stomach cavity, pat them dry and place in a dish. Season with salt and pepper. Sprinkle with the lemon juice and three tablespoons of olive oil and leave to marinate for one hour.

3. Meanwhile, mash the 2 hard-boiled egg yolks with the preserved anchovy fillets and the basil and moisten the resulting purée with one tablespoon of wine vinegar.

4. Drain the fresh marinated anchovies and whisk the marinade into the anchovy paste (3). Season with pepper and add a little more lemon juice or vinegar if necessary.

FINISHING AND SERVING THE SALAD
5. You will now have 8 anchovy fillets and seven strips of red pepper for each person. Arrange them on four plates in overlapping radiating spokes, like a bicycle wheel. Trim the pepper strips to the required length if they are too long.

6. Immediately before serving, pour or spoon the sauce (4) round the peppers and anchovies and accompany with hot toasted bread.

* This salad can also be served with a simple vinaigrette made of olive oil and lemon.

Salade moulée aux écrevisses en trompe-l'oeil
Surprise Salad

Preparation time: 2 hours

For four people

1 kg (2¼ lb) (about 32) freshwater crayfish (écrevisses)
1 large and long carrot
4 large ripe tomatoes
100 g (3½ oz) small young French beans
1 curly endive
3 tablespoons walnut oil
1 tablespoon wine vinegar
1 teaspoon Dijon mustard
8 tablespoons crème fraîche (double cream)
juice of 2 lemons
1 sprig of chervil *or* basil
salt, freshly ground pepper
Special equipment: 4 round non-fluted pastry cutters 4¾" in diameter
 and ¾" deep

PREPARING THE CRAYFISH AND VEGETABLES
1. Remove the little black intestine of the crayfish by pulling the central fin away sharply. Rinse the crayfish under cold running water in a sieve and then plunge into boiling salted water for 3 minutes. Remove them and shell the tails. Set aside. (Keep the shells to make the crayfish oil described on page 46.)

2. Have ready a fresh pan of boiling salted water. Peel the carrot. Cut it lengthwise into 8 identical strips ⅛" thick, ¾" wide and 6" long. Plunge the strips into boiling water for 1 minute and refresh in iced water. Drain, and dry on a cloth or paper towels.

3. Plunge the tomatoes into the boiling water for 15 seconds and then peel with the help of a sharp knife. Halve them and remove all the seeds. Chop the flesh very very finely. Put to drain in a sieve over a bowl so that the juices can run out.

4. Trim the beans and cook them in the boiling water so they are just crunchy. Plunge them in iced water, cut them in half and set them aside.

5. Pick over and wash the curly endive, and break it into small sprigs. Only the yellow middle part is needed for this salad. Remove any tough stalks. Make a vinaigrette with the oil, vinegar and mustard, seasoned with salt and pepper.

6. Place a pastry cutter in the middle of each plate to act as a mould. Dip the strips of carrot (2) in the vinaigrette (5) and place the two, end to end, round the interior edge of each mould, trimming them if necessary.

7. Mix together the shelled tails of the crayfish, the salad and the beans in a bowl, and dress with the vinaigrette (5). Mix well, and season with salt and pepper if necessary and drain off any excess vinaigrette. Pack this salad firmly into the mould, pressing it down with the back of a fork, and finish with a layer of chopped raw tomato (3). Season with salt and pepper and smooth over with a palette knife, so that the tomato is level with the top of the mould. Mop up any sauce which has escaped under the bottom edge of the mould. Very carefully, ease off the moulds so that you are left with four "trompe-l'oeil" gâteaux, apparently made of carrot and garnished with tomato purèe.

SERVING THE GATEAUX
8. Mix the cream and the lemon juice in a bowl and season with salt and pepper. Pour this cream round the carrot gâteaux. Place a little sprig of chervil or a basil leaf in the centre of each and serve immediately.

* If you do not have the pastry cutters you can use strips of clean card stapled into circles.

"Une salade sous forme de devinette."

Papillon de sardines fraîches
Sardine "Butterflies"

Preparation time: 1½ hours

For four people

12 fresh sardines
1 red pepper
250 ml (scant half pint) olive oil
250 ml (scant half pint) crème fraîche (double cream)
1 leaf of gelatine
2 small courgettes
2 large cultivated mushrooms
1 bunch of chives
1 black olive
1 tablespoon of white wine vinegar
salt, freshly ground pepper

PREPARING THE SARDINES

1. Scale, behead and clean the sardines, and rinse under running water. Using your fingers, ease the fillets away from the backbone of each sardine. Sprinkle with salt and pepper and set the fillets aside.

MAKING THE PURÉE OF RED PEPPER AND THE GARNISH

2. Heat 5 tablespoons of olive oil until it is very hot indeed and roll the pepper in it for approximately 1 minute. Drain, and when it has cooled somewhat, remove the skin with the help of a sharp knife, halve the pepper and remove the seeds and white fibres.

3. Blend the skinned pepper to a smooth purée with 6 tablespoons of oil. Season with salt and pepper. Pour into a bowl and chill until the purée has become firm (a basin full of ice cubes will save time). Put four serving plates in the refrigerator.

4. While the pepper purée is chilling, slice the courgettes and mushrooms finely, then chop them and fry them rapidly in a tablespoon of olive oil. Remove and drain the vegetables while they are still crisp. Soften the gelatine in a little cold water for 10 minutes.

5. Whisk the cream until it is stiff and fold it, together with the drained, softened gelatine, into the chilled pepper purée.

66

6. Using a wetted tablespoon, shape four quenelles (little sausage shapes) from the pepper purée (5). Place one in the middle of each chilled serving plate to make the "bodies" of the butterflies and return the plates to the refrigerator immediately.

7. Heat 1 tablespoon of olive oil in a sauté pan. When it starts to smoke, fry the sardine fillets (1) very quickly for 5 seconds on each side. Remove and drain on paper towels.

8. Take the plates out of the refrigerator again and form a flat circle of courgettes and mushrooms on each side of the "body" – about one tablespoon to each circle. Put three sardine fillets, skin side up, on each circle at angles to the "body" to complete the "wings". Arrange chives to represent the "antennae". The eyes can be fashioned from little pieces of black olive.

FINISHING AND SERVING THE "BUTTERFLIES"

9. Make a vinaigrette in the usual way with 3 tablespoons olive oil, 1 tablespoon of wine vinegar, salt and pepper. Sprinkle each sardine fillet with this dressing and serve immediately.

* These "butterflies" can also, of course, be made with fresh anchovies. For the visual effect to succeed, each "butterfly" must be made separately.

"Un peu d'ingéniosité, de réflexion, un papillon est né. Bien d'autres choses encore peuvent émerger de votre imagination."

Bûches d'écrevisses au saumon fumé
Crayfish in Jelly with Smoked Salmon

Preparation time: 2 hours plus six hours chilling

For four people

32 freshwater crayfish or Dublin Bay prawns
6 tablespoons olive oil
1 shallot
2 cloves of garlic, crushed
1 leaf gelatine
200 g (7 oz) smoked salmon, in four slices
fresh tarragon
pepper
200 g (7 oz) mixed salad leaves
2 tablespoons vinaigrette sauce

For the Sauce
250 ml (scant pint) double cream or crème fraîche
2 hard-boiled eggs
15 g (½ oz) each of fresh chervil, tarragon, parsley, and basil, chopped
juice of 1 lemon
cayenne pepper
salt, freshly ground pepper

"Un 'aspic' facile à réaliser à la portée de tous."

COOKING THE CRAYFISH

1. Remove the black intestine from each crayfish. The fresher the crayfish, the easier this is, but it takes a lot of practice.

2. Heat 4 tablespoons of the olive oil in a large cast-iron casserole until it smokes, then throw in the crayfish and fry them over a fairly brisk heat turning them carefully. When they have all turned red, remove them with a slotted spoon, throwing out the oil. Remove the heads. Soften the chopped shallot and crushed garlic in a little fresh olive oil in the same casserole and throw in the heads of the crayfish. Cover with water and simmer for approximately 1 hour.

MAKING THE CRAYFISH JELLY

3. Strain this stock into another saucepan and reduce until you have about 250 ml (scant ½ pint) of rather strong stock. Soften the gelatine in cold water and add to the hot stock. Stir until it has melted completely and set the pan on one side to cool.

FILLING THE MOULDS

4. Take four small long cylindrical moulds and line each with a slice of smoked salmon. Shell the crayfish tails and divide them between the moulds. Sprinkle with a little fresh tarragon and pour in the cooled but still liquid stock (3). Fold the smoked salmon over the top so that the crayfish and their jelly is entirely enclosed. Chill in the refrigerator for 6 hours.

MAKING THE SAUCE

5. Whip the cream until it has doubled in volume. Liquidise the hard-boiled eggs with the fresh herbs. Add the lemon juice to give the necessary acidity. Fold in the whipped cream and season with cayenne, salt and pepper.

FINISHING AND SERVING THE JELLIED CRAYFISH

Turn out each mould on a plate putting on the one side a generous spoonful of sauce and on the other a little bouquet of mixed salad leaves dressed with vinaigrette.

* The moulds are those used by charcutiers for making ham moulds. You could use small petits suisses moulds instead, but you would need 16, as each one will only hold 2 crayfish tails.

Salade de pigeons aux amandes et mousse de champignons
Pigeon Salad with Almonds and Mushroom Mousse

Preparation time: 1 hour and 3 hours setting time

For four people

300 g (10½ oz) mushrooms
100 g (3½ oz) butter
juice of half a lemon
150 ml (¼ pint) walnut oil
4 pigeons
24 fresh green almonds or 50 g (1¾ oz) split almonds
200 g (7 oz) lamb's lettuce (mâche)
1 tablespoon wine vinegar
1 teaspoon Dijon mustard
salt, freshly ground pepper
1 shallot, very finely chopped

PRELIMINARY PREPARATIONS

1. Trim and wash the mushrooms. Cut them into quarters and cook for 5 minutes in half the butter, 1 tablespoon water, the lemon juice, salt and pepper.

2. Drain the mushrooms and liquidise them while still hot, with 3-4 tablespoons walnut oil, to obtain a smooth creamy mousse. Pour into a glass bowl and chill over ice or in the refrigerator for 3 hours.

3. Meanwhile, remove the breasts and legs from the birds and trim the fillets of their skin and fibres. Slit the meatiest part of the legs so that they cook evenly.

4. If you are using fresh almonds, cut each in half, remove the kernel and peel off the brown skin. Pick over the mâche and wash briefly in cold water. Drain carefully. Make a vinaigrette with the rest of the walnut oil, the wine vinegar, mustard and salt and pepper.

COOKING THE PIGEONS

5. Heat the remaining butter in a sauté pan or frying pan and cook the legs for 7-8 minutes. Add the breasts and cook them for 30 seconds on each side, so they are still rosy inside. Drain the thighs and breasts and slice the breasts thinly.

FINISHING AND SERVING THE SALAD

6. Using a wet spoon, form the mushroom mousse into 8 quenelle shapes and place two on each plate in a V-shape. Decorate each quenelle with the halved almonds and lay a sliced breast over each one. Fill the Vs with a little bunch of mâche leaves dressed with a little of the walnut vinaigrette and arrange the legs across the top. Sprinkle the sliced breasts with a little very finely chopped shallot. Just before serving, give each plate a good grinding of black pepper and coat the breasts very lightly with a little vinaigrette.

* Using split almonds instead of fresh almonds makes this recipe easier to achieve but the taste will be rather different.
* To open fresh almonds, split them lengthwise with a knife or give them a sharp tap with a small hammer.
* Some slices of toasted French bread, spread with the mashed cooked livers of the pigeons, would go well with this salad.

Brandade de soles glacée aux truffes
Chilled Sole Mousse with Truffles

Preparation time: 2 hours plus 6 hours chilling time

For four people
1 large potato, in its skin
6 fillets of sole
300 ml (½ pint) double cream or crème fraîche
1 clove of garlic
40 g (1½ oz) black truffles
6-7 tablespoons olive oil
3 leaves gelatine
salt, pepper

"Toute la Provence dans ces quenelles qui constituent une excellente entrée."

1. Boil the potato, in its skin, in a pan of salted water for 45 minutes.

2. Rinse the fillets of sole and pat them dry. Bring 2 tablespoons of the cream to the boil with 250 ml (scant ½ pint) cold water and season with salt and pepper. Plunge in the fillets and immediately turn off the heat. Cover the pan and set aside in a warm place until the potato is ready.

3. Peel the garlic and crush it to a smooth paste. Chop the truffles finely and spread them out on a large plate. Chill in the refrigerator.

MAKING THE MOUSSE
4. Peel the cooked potato while it is still hot, cut it in four and place in the bowl of a food processor. Add the sole fillets, reserving the cooking liquid, with 3 tablespoons olive oil, salt and pepper and purée till smooth.

5. Soften 3 leaves of gelatine in cold water and then dissolve in 6-7 tablespoons of the liquid in which the sole fillets have cooked (2). Add the crushed garlic (3), fold the liquid into the purée (4) and remove to a bowl and allow to cool.

6. Meanwhile, whip the remaining cream until it is firm. Fold in the cooled purée with a spatula and chill for approximately six hours.

FINISHING AND SERVING THE MOUSSE
7. Using two wet tablespoons, form the chilled sole mousse into 8 handsome quenelles and roll each one carefully in the chopped truffles (3), working very quickly. Arrange 2 quenelles on each plate and return to the refrigerator until you are ready to serve the mousse. Accompany with slices of French bread toasted and rubbed with garlic.

* You can replace the truffles with black olives. And why not? But what a difference.

Rognonnade de lapereau aux aubergines
Rabbit Terrine with Aubergines

Preparation time: 3 hours plus 12 hours chilling time
Oven temperature: 450°F/340°C/Gas 8

For four to
six people

2 saddles of rabbit
8 rabbit kidneys with their covering of fat
1 rabbit liver
200 g (7½ oz) fresh wild mushrooms, or 50 g (2 oz) dried
4 tablespoons olive oil
a deep pan of vegetable oil for frying the aubergines
100 g (3½ oz) butter
3 aubergines
1 shallot, finely chopped
1 tablespoon red wine vinegar
1 sprig basil, chopped
1 clove of garlic
salt, freshly ground pepper

PRELIMINARY PREPARATIONS

THE DAY BEFORE
1. Remove the bones from the saddles, keeping the fillets
attached to each other. Flatten the side flaps attached to the
fillets with a cleaver and season with salt and pepper.

2. Clean the mushrooms, chop them coarsely and fry rapidly in
very hot olive oil. Drain them and chop them very finely. Melt
50 g (1½ oz) butter in a sauté pan and add the chopped
mushrooms. Cook, stirring continually with a wooden spoon,
over a medium heat until all the mushroom juices have
evaporated. If using dried mushrooms soak them first for 20
minutes in warm water, then squeeze them dry and proceed as
before.

3. Chop the rabbit liver very finely, and away from the heat,
add to the hot mushrooms. Allow to cool.

4. Cut the aubergines in half lengthwise. Make diagonal cuts in
the flesh and fry very quickly in hot vegetable oil. Drain off
excess oil, remove the flesh and use the skins to line a long
narrow buttered cake tin 10″ by 3″. Reserve the aubergine
purée.

74

5. Season the rabbit kidneys, still covered with protective layer of fat, and fry, together with the chopped shallot in 30 g (1 oz) butter. Drain and allow to cool. Pre-heat the oven.

STUFFING THE SADDLES
6. Spread out the boned saddles (1) and spread with a thin layer of the mushroom-liver mixture (3). Place 4 kidneys on each saddle and season with salt and pepper.

MAKING THE TERRINE
Fold over the flaps and place the two stuffed saddles in the terrine taking care not to disturb the lining. Press the saddles down lightly and add 2 teaspoons of water. Fold the aubergine skins over the top to enclose the stuffed saddles. Cover with foil and then with a lid and cook in a hot oven for 1¾ hours.

7. When the terrine is cooked, place it under a weight until it has become quite cold, and chill in the refrigerator for 12 hours before serving.

FINISHING AND SERVING THE TERRINE
8. Just before serving, turn out the terrine on to a serving dish, taking care not to puncture the purple "coat". Slice with a sharp knife and serve on individual plates. Accompany with the aubergine purée, mixed with 1 tablespoon olive oil, the vinegar, basil, a hint of garlic, salt and pepper. A few slices of grilled french bread sprinkled with thyme, and there is your dish ready to eat, smelling deliciously of the Niçoise countryside.

* It is best if you ask your butcher or game dealer to bone the saddles for you.
* You can use a veal kidney instead of the rabbit kidneys.

"Une terrine de lapin dont les bardes traditionnelles sont remplacées par un habit violet."

Persillé de langouste rose et de ris de veau
Terrine of Crawfish and Sweetbreads with Herbs

Preparation time: 3½ hours, plus 24 hours chilling
Oven temperature: 400°F/200°C/Gas 6

For from
eight to
ten people

2 sets of veal sweetbreads
white part of 1 leek, chopped
2 shallots, chopped
1 tomato, skinned and seeded and chopped
1 stick celery, chopped
500 g (1 lb 2 oz) carrots
100 g (3½ oz) butter
2 tablespoons olive oil
1 crawfish of about 800 g (1 lb 12 oz)
250 ml (scant ½ pint) dry white wine
20 g (⅔ oz) each of chopped fresh parsley, tarragon, chervil, chives
    and basil
100 g (3½ oz) boned chicken breast
200 g (7 oz) whipping cream
salt, freshly ground pepper

PREPARING THE SWEETBREADS
1. Soak the sweetbreads in cold water to remove the blood and
then poach for 15 minutes. Rinse in cold water and drain. Skin
them, taking care to remove the fibres and fatty parts. Cut into
dice the size of a sugar lump and set aside.

PREPARING THE CRAWFISH
2. Put the chopped leek, shallots, tomato, the celery and two
chopped carrots in a large heavy pan with the oil and butter and
brown lightly over a medium heat. When the vegetables are
becoming tender, throw in the crawfish quickly, moisten with
the wine and a glass of water, season with salt and pepper, cover
with a lid and cook over a medium heat for 20 minutes, turning
the crawfish once. When it is cooked, remove and drain the
crawfish, strain the cooking liquid and reduce by half. Shell the
crawfish and cut the flesh into dice the same size as the sweetbreads.

MAKING THE STUFFING
3. In a large bowl, mix the sweetbreads, crawfish and chopped

herbs together. Add the reduced cooking liquid and set aside in a cool place.

4. Purée the raw chicken in a blender or food processor, then add all the cream at once. Blend briefly, season with salt and pepper and add to the mixture in the bowl. Mix carefully with a wooden spoon.

LINING THE TERRINE

5. Preheat the oven. Cut the remaining carrots into lengthwise strips the thickness of a potato crisp. Cook them in boiling salted water until they are just "al dente". Drain and refresh them, drain again and pat dry.

FINISHING THE TERRINE

6. Butter an 8″ rectangular terrine and line it with strips of cooked carrot. Fill with the sweetbread and crawfish mixture and cover with a sheet of buttered foil. Place in a roasting tin half-filled with water and cook in the oven for 45 minutes. Remove from the oven, cool completely and chill for 24 hours. Turn out onto a serving dish, after running a knife round the sides of the terrine and dipping it briefly in hot water.

* A meat-slicer will enable you to cut the carrot strips perfectly evenly.

"Un persillé de 'bourgogne' enrichi mais surtout plus sophistiqué."

Salade de tomates et de queues d'écrevisses à la crème
Tomato and Crayfish Salad

Preparation time: 2 hours

For four people

60 freshwater crayfish *or* Dublin Bay Prawns
1 carrot, finely chopped
1 white part of leek, split lengthways
1 onion, chopped
8 peppercorns
1 stick of celery
1 litre (1¾ pints) dry white wine
4 tablespoons red wine vinegar
a sprig of fresh thyme
1 bayleaf
4 handsome tomatoes
250 ml (scant ½ pint) double cream or crème fraîche
a sprig of fresh tarragon, chopped
100 g (3½ oz) lamb's lettuce (mâche)
salt, freshly ground pepper

PREPARING AND COOKING THE CRAYFISH
1. Remove the black intestine from each crayfish. Wash them in running water, and drain.

2. Bring 3 litres (5¼ pints) cold water to the boil with the chopped carrot, leek and onion, peppercorns and celery. Add salt generously, and add the wine, 2 tablespoons of wine vinegar, thyme and bayleaf. Let this court-bouillon simmer for 15 minutes. Plunge in the crayfish, cover and boil for 10 minutes. Remove the crayfish with a slotted spoon.

PREPARING THE TOMATOES
3. Bring the liquid to the boil once more and plunge in the tomatoes, from which you have removed the stalks, for 10 seconds. Refresh in cold water and remove the skins. Cut each tomato in eight equal sections, joined at the base. Open out this "crown" and remove the flesh and seeds with a teaspoon. You will have four empty tomato flowers each with 8 petals, which should be set aside.

DRESSING THE CRAYFISH
4. Remove the crayfish heads and shell the tails.

5. Mix the cream, chopped tarragon and 2 tablespoons red wine vinegar in a bowl and season with salt and pepper. Stir in the crayfish tails and let them absorb the flavours of the sauce.

FINISHING AND SERVING THE TOMATO AND CRAYFISH SALADS
6. Arrange a fringe of mâche leaves round the edges of 4 plates and place a tomato in the middle of each, opening out the "petals" carefully. Just before serving, spoon the crayfish in their sauce into each tomato and serve chilled.

* The tomatoes must be perfectly ripe.
* You can use a few crayfish heads as decoration.

"Une fleur pas encore répertoriée par les jardiniers."

Salade de saint-pierre *"sauce gaspacho"*
John Dory Salad with a "Gazpacho" Sauce

Preparation time: 30 minutes plus 2 hours chilling

For four people

3 cloves of garlic, peeled
2 eggs
250 ml (scant ½ pint) olive oil
1 small cucumber
250 g (9 oz) ripe red tomatoes
2 tablespoons red wine vinegar
250 ml (scant ½ pint) still mineral water
500 g (1 lb 2 oz) fillets of John Dory *or* other firm white fish
salt, freshly ground pepper

MAKING THE "GAZPACHO" SAUCE

1. Purée the garlic and liquidise with the eggs, olive oil, salt and pepper to obtain a mayonnaise.

2. Peel and seed the cucumber. Remove the stalks of the tomatoes. Pass both through a juice extractor and whisk the strained juice into the mayonnaise. Add the vinegar and mineral water and chill thoroughly for approximately 2 hours.

COOKING AND SERVING THE JOHN DORY

3. Meanwhile, slice the fish fillets in about 20 small, very thin escalopes and season with salt and pepper.

4. Just before you want to eat, heat a non-stick pan and cook the escalopes very quickly, turning them once and taking care not to overcook them. Pat carefully with paper towels and arrange 5 or 6 on each plate. Pour round a ladleful of the "gazpacho" sauce and serve immediately.

* The fish escalopes can also be arranged on a bed of crisp lettuce cut into strips.

"Une salade tiède de poisson blanc, une sauce très particulière qui rappellera les vacances espagnoles."

Terrine d'aubergines aux anchois
Aubergine Terrine with Anchovies

Preparation time: 1 hour plus 6 hours chilling time

or from six
to eight
people

12 fresh anchovies
juice of 2 lemons
a pinch of curry powder
4 tablespoons olive oil
2 aubergines
2 leaves fresh basil, chopped
1 clove of garlic, puréed
10 g (⅓ oz) fish aspic dissolved in 250 ml (scant ½ pint) water
salt, freshly ground pepper

1. Remove the heads from the anchovies and remove the fillets from the backbones with the fingers. Rinse in cold running water and pat dry. Let them marinate for 30 minutes with the juice of 1 lemon, 2 tablespoons olive oil, the curry powder, a very little salt and freshly ground black pepper.

2. Meanwhile, prepare the aubergines. Cut them in half lengthwise, sprinkle with a little olive oil and bake for 15 minutes on a baking sheet in a very hot oven. The heat will blacken the skins: when they have cooled remove the flesh with a spoon. Mash it thoroughly in a wooden salad bowl, and then gradually add the rest of the olive oil in a thin stream, mashing all the time. Add the basil, cooled fish aspic, the juice of the second lemon and pepper, and mix well.

3. Remove the anchovy fillets from the marinade and pat them dry. Line a long narrow terrine with the fillets, pour in the aubergine mixture, smoothing it down well, and put in the refrigerator. Chill for a minimum of 6 hours and then turn out carefully on to an oblong plate. Serve with toasted bread and a mixed green salad dressed with lemon juice.

* When you turn out the terrine, take care to cut between the anchovy fillets, or you will waste all your hard work.

"Un bûche qui surprendra vos amis, même si ce n'est pas Noël."

Confit de pigeon aux olives noires
Pigeon Terrine with Black Olives

Preparation time: 5 hours plus 12 hours chilling
Oven temperature: 225°F/110°C/Gas ¼

For four people

2 plump farm-bred pigeons of 500 g (1 lb 2 oz) each
2-3 tablespoons peanut oil
200 g (7 oz) raw duck foie gras, sliced
4 fresh cèpes
4 fresh chanterelles
1 tablespoon olive oil
30 small black Niçois olives
2 cloves of garlic, peeled and chopped
1 tablespoon Armagnac
1 tablespoon parsley, chopped
1 bayleaf
a small sprig of fresh thyme
salt, freshly ground pepper

1. Singe and gut the birds if this has not already been done. Cut each in half and brown them in very hot oil for about 1 minute. Let them cool, then drain and remove the bones, leaving those in the wings and the legs.

2. Brown the foie gras briefly without extra fat, in a very hot pan. Drain off any fat that runs out.

3. Clean the wild mushrooms and rinse briefly under running water. Fry them in 1 tablespoon olive oil until they have given off their liquid, and drain.

4. You are now ready to assemble the "Confit". Preheat the oven. Have ready an oval earthenware terrine with a lid and put in at random the pieces of pigeon, the foie gras, the mushrooms and the olives. Season with a little salt and pepper and add the garlic, Armagnac, parsley, bayleaf and a small pinch of fresh thyme. Pour in enough cold water to cover all the ingredients and seal with a sheet of foil and the lid. Cook in a bain-marie in a very low oven for 4 hours. Allow to cool, and then chill in the refrigerator for 12 hours before serving.

* A salad of bitter leaves such as arugula or radicchio – served with croûtons rubbed with garlic – is the perfect accompaniment.

"Confit d'origine du Sud-Ouest, qui ne sera que meilleur après quelques jours d'attente avant de le déguster."

Omelette froide "belle niçoise"
Cold Omelette "Belle Niçoise"

Preparation time: 2 hours plus 5-6 hours chilling
Oven temperature: 400°F/200°C/Gas 6

For from
four to six
people

1 medium aubergine
1 slender courgette
200 ml (⅓ pint) olive oil
1 red and 1 green pepper
1 onion
6 eggs
1 sprig fresh basil, chopped
1 clove of garlic, chopped
2 tomatoes, skinned, seeded and diced
salt, freshly ground pepper
fresh lemon juice

1. Without peeling them, cut the aubergine and the courgette in fine lengthwise strips. Heat a little of the olive oil in a frying pan until it is very hot and brown the strips lightly. Remove excess oil by patting with paper towels and line a small cake tin with overlapping alternate strips of the two vegetables.

2. Cut the peppers and onion into small dice and soften in 3 tablespoons of olive oil over a low heat. Drain and allow to cool. Preheat the oven.

3. Beat the six eggs in a bowl with a fork and add the peppers and onions, the chopped basil and garlic and the diced tomato. Pour this mixture into the lined mould.

4. Cover with a sheet of foil and cook in a bain-marie for 1¾ hours in the oven. Allow to chill for 5-6 hours and turn out. Cut into fine slices and cover with a very thin sheen of olive oil and lemon juice.

* Check that the omelette is cooked right through, by inserting a skewer or sharp knife before taking it out of the oven.

"Il s'agit d'une ratatouille niçoise additionnée d'oeufs battus dont le montage se fait en moule préalablement tapissé de lames de courgettes et d'aubergines."

Gratin chaud de carottes, sauce vichy-citron
Hot Carrot Gratin with a Lemon Sauce

Preparation time: 2 hours
Oven temperature: 475°F/240°C/Gas 9

For six to eight people

500 g (1 lb 2 oz) carrots
1 litre (1¾ pints) Vichy water
275 g (9½ oz) butter
8 tablespoons fresh lemon juice
7 tablespoons crème fraîche
3 leaves of gelatine
6 egg yolks
6 egg whites
25 g (1 oz) flour
1 tablespoon chopped chives
salt, freshly ground pepper

"Un gratin 'aimable' qui a la consistance d'un soufflé."

1. Scrape the carrots with a potato-peeler and process approximately two thirds of them through the juice extracting fitment of a food-processor. You should have 8 tablespoons of carrot juice. Discard the pulp.

2. Chop the remaining carrots finely and put them in a sauté pan with Vichy water to cover. Dot with 100 g (3½ oz) of diced butter, season with salt and pepper, cover with foil and cook on a low heat until the liquid has almost completely evaporated. Meanwhile, have ready the fresh lemon juice. Reserve 1 tablespoon. Mix the rest with the carrot juice (1) and the cream and bring to the boil in a large saucepan. Put the gelatine to soak in cold water.

3. Preheat the oven to its highest setting. Mix the egg yolks and the flour together in a bowl, and whisk in the boiling juice-cream mixture. Return the mixture to the saucepan and bring back to the boil. Season with salt and pepper and stir in the soaked and squeezed gelatine so that it dissolves thoroughly. Pour the mixture into a large bowl. Fold in the cooked carrots (2). Whip the egg whites with a little salt to a snow and fold them in.

4. Butter a gratin dish lavishly, and pour in the carrot mixture. Cook for 10 minutes in the very hot oven and finish off by browning briefly under the grill.

5. Meanwhile, bring 7 tablespoons of Vichy water to the boil and whisk in 150 g (5¼ oz) diced butter, the reserved tablespoon of lemon juice. Season with salt and pepper and add the chopped chives. Pour into a heated sauceboat and serve as soon as the gratin is ready.

* Do not whip the egg whites too firmly. If they are still moist they will mix more satisfactorily with the cream.

Feuilleté d'asperges, sauce germiny
Asparagus Pastries with Sorrel Sauce

Preparation time: 1½ hours
Oven temperatures: 450°F/230°C/Gas 8

For four people

32 sticks of slender green asparagus
200 g (7 oz) fresh or frozen puff pastry
1 egg, beaten
100 g (3½ oz) fresh sorrel
3 egg yolks
3 tablespoons crème fraîche
100 g (3½ oz) butter
salt, freshly ground pepper

"Deux goûts 'sauvages': l'amertume de l'asperge et l'acidité de l'oseille; un mélange puissant dont l'ardeur est atténuée par la crème et les oeufs."

1. Pare the asparagus with a potato-peeler and trim to approximately six inches long (including the tips). Wash under cold running water and blanch in boiling salted water. Refresh as quickly as possible under cold running water and drain. Preheat the oven.

2. Butter a sauté pan lavishly and lay the asparagus in it. Add water to cover and season with salt and pepper. Cover with a sheet of foil and cook gently for about 15 minutes. Remove from the heat and keep hot.

3. Meanwhile, roll out the pastry and cut four ovals, using a card template or a pastry cutter. Brush the upper side of each oval with beaten egg, decorate with a fork and bake for 7 minutes.

4. Trim and wash the sorrel in plenty of cold water. Shred it very finely and soften – without butter or oil and stirring continually – in a small non-stick pan. Remove the sorrel to a bowl.

5. Whisk the egg yolks and the cream together in a bowl.

6. When the pastries are cooked, cut thin layers off the upper sides to serve as lids and hollow out the interiors with a fork. Keep them hot.

7. Remove the asparagus from the sauté pan (2), drain them and divide them between the pastry cases. Bring the liquid in which the asparagus has cooked to the boil, and add the sorrel. Pour the boiling liquid on to the egg-cream mixture, stir and return to the pan. Heat without boiling, to thicken the yolks.

8. Put each pastry on a hot plate and pour a little sauce over the asparagus. Just before serving, put on the pastry lids.

* If you can find asparagus with purplish tips it is the best in the world. Mine comes from Paul Rudel of Roquette-sur-Siagne.

Courgettes à la fleur et aux truffes
Truffled Courgettes

Preparation time: 3 hours
Oven temperature: 400°F/200°C/Gas 6

For four people

16 courgettes very fresh and with their flowers attached
10 tablespoons olive oil
a bunch of basil, chervil, and tarragon
2 eggs
50 g (1¾ oz) fine breadcrumbs
7 tablespoons double cream
250 ml (scant half pint) whipping cream
40 g (1½ oz) preserved truffle, sliced, and 1 teaspoon juice from the jar or can
150 g (5¼ oz) cold diced butter
salt, freshly ground pepper

1. Trim the courgettes so that the flowers are attached to four inches of courgette. Peel them with a potato-peeler and plunge into boiling salted water for 5-10 seconds to blanch and soften the flowers. Refresh in iced water, drain and set aside. Soak the breadcrumbs in the whipping cream.

2. Soften the courgette peelings in olive oil, and pour into the bowl of a mixer or food-processor. Add ten leaves from the basil, the eggs and the breadcrumbs and cream. Season with salt and pepper and mix to a smooth purée. Chill for a few minutes.

3. Preheat the oven and have ready an oiled baking sheet sprinkled with salt and pepper. Pack the purée into a forcing bag with a nozzle.

4. One person, using the index fingers and thumbs of both hands, spreads out the flower very, very carefully, and inflates it by blowing gently into it. At that moment the second person uses the forcing bag to pipe the purée into the flower so that it is three quarters full. The first then twists the flower so that the ends of the petals form a natural knot, sealing in the stuffing. Repeat this process with each courgette and lay them on the prepared baking sheet. Sprinkle with a little olive oil and bake for 40 minutes.

5. Meanwhile, remove the stalks from the herbs and slice the truffle finely. Bring 7 tablespoons of water to the boil with a

pinch of salt and a little pepper and whisk in the cold diced butter. Remove from the heat, add the slices of truffle and the truffle juice and leave to infuse in a warm place. Separately, whip the double cream and chill.

6. Sponge excess oil from the cooked courgettes and arrange four in a star on each of four large hot plates. Remove the slices of truffle from the sauce and divide them between the four plates. Bring the sauce to the boil, simmer for a minute or so and fold in the whipped cream. Check the seasoning and pour over the courgettes. Sprinkle with the fresh herbs and serve immediately.

* The truffle sauce can be replaced with an olive oil and tomato sauce similar to that described on page 113.

Editor's note The courgettes for this spectacular dish need to be so fresh, and their flowers so unwilted, that they are best picked from your own or a friend's garden unless you have access, as Jacques Maximin does in the South of France, to an exceptional vegetable grower. The stuffing of the flowers can most easily be done by two people working together.

"Grâce au courage, à l'expérience de la famille Auda de Carros, installée au Plan de Gattières, qui produit cette qualité de courgettes unique au monde, j'ai pu réaliser cette recette que je considère comme un très grand plat, anoblissant ainsi le légume de base de la cuisine du comté de Nice: le courgette."

Papillote d'artichauts violets
Artichokes with Langoustines and Foie Gras

Preparation time: 1½ hours
Oven temperature: 450°F/250°C/Gas 8

For four
people

4 large artichokes
white part of a leek
1 medium carrot, peeled
4 langoustines
120 g (4¼ oz) raw duck foie gras
120 g (4¼ oz) butter
salt, freshly ground pepper

"Artichauts, langoustines, foie gras, un tiercé audacieux et surprenant de
saveurs."

1. Remove the stalks from the artichokes and bring them to the boil in a large pan of salted water. Cook them for approximately 45 minutes, depending on the variety and their freshness.

2. Meanwhile, cut the leek and carrot into fine julienne strips. Cook the strips in boiling salt water until they are al dente. Refresh under cold running water and drain.

3. Remove the shells from the shellfish. Season with salt and freshly ground pepper.

4. Cut the foie gras into four equal slices, and fry each slice for 30 seconds on each side. Sprinkle with a very little salt and drain.

5. When the cooked artichokes are cool enough to handle, remove all the leaves and the fibrous choke. Divide the julienne vegetables between the four artichoke hearts, top with a langoustine and a slice of foie gras and 1 tablespoon of butter to each heart.

6. Preheat the oven. Have ready 2 pieces of kitchen foil 12 inches by 8 inches. Place the stuffed artichoke hearts on one sheet, cover with the other and fold over the edges to create a hermetically sealed package. Just before you make the final seal, pour in a wineglass of water. Place the foil packages in a shallow oven dish containing half an inch of hot water (this will speed up the cooking process). Bake for 15 minutes.

7. Serve the papillote on a warmed serving dish and open the foil wrapping in front of your guests. It looks and smells spectacular.

* A good sprig of fresh tarragon adds extra flavour to the papillote.

Petites tomates farcies au maigre de chèvre
Tomatoes stuffed with Goats' Cheese

Preparation time: 2 hours
Oven temperature: 400°F/200°C/Gas 6

For four people

16 small tomatoes weighing 50 g (1¾ oz) each, with their stalks if
    possible
1 onion
2 medium sized fresh goats' cheeses, well drained
1 courgette
1 aubergine
1 red and 1 green pepper
7 tablespoons olive oil
250 ml (scant half pint) whipping cream
100 g (3½ oz) cold butter, diced
a sprig of basil, shredded
salt, freshly ground pepper

"Un marriage réussi dont l'examen de passage fut réalisé lors d'une émission télevisée, 'Antenne 2 Midi' dont j'étais l'invité du jour, le 14 août 1981."

92

1. Bring a pan of salted water to the boil and plunge in the tomatoes for 10 seconds, removing them immediately to ice-cold water. Peel them with a sharp knife, taking care not to detach the stalk. Slice off the stalk end to form a little "lid", of which the stalk will form the handle. Using your little finger, scoop out the seeds, if possible without destroying too much of the structure of the tomato. Place the tomatoes upside down on a rack to drain.

2. Meanwhile, make the stuffing. Remove the seeds from the peppers, peel the onion (but not the other vegetables) and chop them finely together. Cook the vegetable dice briefly in olive oil until they are cooked but still crisp. Drain well.

3. Bring the cream to the boil, season with salt and pepper and add three quarters of the shredded basil. Simmer until the cream has reduced by half and is beginning to thicken.

4. Mash the cheeses with a fork and mix them thoroughly into the hot cream. Stir in the drained diced vegetables, cool a little, and place in the refrigerator.

5. When the stuffing is completely cold, preheat the oven. Season the tomatoes with salt and pepper, and fill with the stuffing. Top with their "lids" and arrange in a shallow oven dish with 7 tablespoons of water. Bake for 15 minutes.

6. Remove the tomatoes from the oven dish and arrange on four plates. Keep hot. Pour the cooking liquid into a small pan and bring to the boil. Off the heat, whisk in the diced butter. Check the seasoning, add the remaining shredded basil and pour the sauce round the tomatoes.

* When seeding the tomatoes, it is very important to keep as much of the internal structure of the tomato as possible, so that they do not collapse when they are cooked.

Vinaigrette de filets de rougets en robe de poireaux
Red Mullet wrapped in Leeks

Preparation time: 1½ hours

For four people
10 small red mullet *or* 300 g (10 oz) mullet fillets
2 large leeks, trimmed
20 slices of truffle, weighing approximately 60 g (2 oz)
2 shallots
5 tablespoons olive oil
juice of 2 limes
a small bunch of chervil
salt and freshly ground pepper

"Y sont pas beaux mes rougets?"

1. Remove the fillets from the mullet leaving the skin in place, and pick out as many of the fine bones as possible with tweezers. This requires a great deal of patience. Scrape the scales from the skin under cold running water.

2. Cook the leeks for approximately 30 minutes in boiling salted water. Refresh and drain them and peel off the leaves, keeping only the white ones.

3. Season the fillets with salt and pepper. Put a slice of truffle on the flesh side of each fillet, and wrap each fillet in a jacket of leek.

4. Chop the shallots finely and set aside. Make a vinaigrette with oil, lime juice, salt and pepper. Remove the stalks from the chervil.

5. Steam the fillets over boiling water for 1 minute on each side. Divide them between four hot plates, sprinkle with a little coarse salt and freshly ground pepper and the vinaigrette. Surround with the chopped raw shallot and chervil. Serve immediately.

* Here is a suggestion for real red mullet experts. Sieve the raw livers of the mullets into the vinaigrette. The taste will be extraordinary.

Pointes de salsifis pochées, beurre d'asperges
Salsify with Asparagus Butter

Preparation time: 1 hour

For four people

2 kg (4½ lbs) salsify
juice of 3 lemons
250 g (8¾ oz) fresh green asparagus tips
150 g (5¼ oz) butter
1 tablespoon snipped chives
salt, freshly ground pepper

1. Wash the salsify in warm water and drain them. Peel them with a potato-peeler, taking care to eliminate all the little black eyes, or root ends. Soak them in water and lemon juice and then cut into 4-inch sticks. Tie the sticks in bundles of twelve, securing them with thread, and cook for at least 20 minutes in water acidulated with the juice of a lemon, starting with cold water.

2. Meanwhile, make the asparagus butter. Wash but do not scrape the asparagus tips. Chop them finely and sweat for a few minutes with two tablespoons of butter in a sauté pan. Add 250 ml (scant half pint) of water, cover and cook for 5 minutes. Pour the contents of the pan into a food processor and blend to a fine, rather liquid, purée. Return to a saucepan, over the heat and whisk in the rest of the butter cut into dice to complete the sauce. Check the seasoning and keep hot.

3. Drain the salsify and untie the bundles. Divide the sticks between four hot soup plates. Add the juice of the third lemon and the chives to the asparagus butter, stir and pour over the salsify.

* Choose medium sized salsify as they will be more tender than larger ones.
* If you like, you can cook the salsify "à blanc" by adding a spoonful of flour to the cooking water in step 1.

"Deux légumes qui s'entendent à merveille."

Salmon with Coarse Salt (page 113)

Lobster Fricassée with Fresh Noodles (page 119)

Lamb with a Roulade of Kidneys (page 128)

Pigeon or Squab Ravioli (page 170)

Mimosa de saumon frais
Salmon Mimosa

Preparation time: 45 minutes

For four people
400 g (14 oz) fresh good quality salmon cut in 16 thin slices
whites of 2 hardboiled eggs, chopped
yolks of 2 hardboiled eggs, chopped
4-6 sprigs of parsley, chopped
20 g (⅔ oz) truffle, chopped
5 tablespoons olive oil
juice of 2 lemons
100 g (3½ oz) mixed salad leaves
salt, freshly ground pepper

1. Mix the chopped truffle with the chopped parsley and the chopped hardboiled eggs.

2. Season the salmon slices with salt and pepper and roll them in the truffle-egg mixture. Press them lightly so that the flavours of the mixture penetrate the salmon.

3. Make a vinaigrette with the oil, lemon juice, salt and pepper, and divide the salad leaves between four plates.

4. Steam the salmon slices for 1 minute on each side over boiling water. Arrange the slices on the salad leaves, pour over the vinaigrette and serve at once, with a dish of coarse salt for those who like it.

* The salmon should be cooked very briefly and should still be pink and moist inside.

"Entrée de poisson haute en couleur, aux saveurs bien prononcées."

FISH AND SHELLFISH

Aillade de pommes de terre aux moules
Aillade of Potatoes with Mussels

Preparation time: 1 hour approximately
Oven temperature: 1. 400°F/200°C/Gas 6, 2. 450°F/230°C/Gas 8

For four people

4 large potatoes
30-40 mussels
1 small white onion, chopped
1 tablespoon olive oil
1 large or two small tomatoes, peeled, seeded and diced
20 cloves of garlic
250 ml (scant ½ pint) whipping cream
4 eggs
coarse salt
salt, freshly ground pepper

1. Preheat the oven to medium. Bake the potatoes, in their skins, on a bed of coarse salt for 1 hour. Meanwhile, wash and scrape the mussels.

2. Soften the chopped onion in the olive oil in a large saucepan. Add the mussels and the tomato and cook, covered for approximately 5 minutes. When the mussels have opened, put them in a colander over a bowl to drain. Shell, and keep warm.

3. Peel the cloves of garlic and remove any green sprouts. Blanch in boiling water, 3-4 times, changing the water each time it comes back to the boil, to remove any bitter flavour. Then purée.

4. Reduce the liquid from the mussels by a quarter, add the cream, bring to the boil and allow to reduce and thicken for 10 minutes. Pour this sauce into a bowl, add the mussels and put to cool in the refrigerator.

5. When the potatoes are cooked reset the oven to hot. Using a serrated knife, cut a lengthwise slice from the top of each potato. Hollow out the rest of the potato with a teaspoon, taking care not to break the skin. Sieve the potato pulp into a bowl and mix carefully with the garlic purée (3), the egg yolks, salt and pepper, using a wooden spoon. Beat the egg whites till stiff and fold delicately into the potato mixture.

6. Put a spoonful of mussels (4) into each potato skin and fill to the brim with the potato soufflé mixture. Bake for 10-12 minutes.

Crépinette verte aux huîtres et cristes-marines
Green Oysters with Spinach and Samphire

Preparation time: 30 minutes
Oven temperature: 450°F/230°F/Gas 8

For two people

12 large oysters
12 large spinach leaves
1 tomato
60 g (2 oz) butter
4 tablespoons olive oil
2 lemons
50 g (1¾ oz) samphire (fresh or pickled)
finely ground pepper
a quantity of coarse salt

PREPARING THE OYSTERS

1. Preheat the oven to its hottest setting.

2. Open the oysters and drain them. Keep the shells.

3. Remove the tough lower stems from the spinach and blanch the leaves for a few seconds in boiling salted water. Refresh and spread out on a cloth to drain.

4. Plunge the tomato into boiling water for 10 seconds and then into iced water. Peel, seed and cut into small dice.

5. Season the oysters with pepper and wrap each in a spinach leaf. Put each parcel into an oyster shell and top with a generous nut of butter. Sprinkle with olive oil and a few samphire tips and finish with a few tomato dice. Cover with the other halves of the shells.

COOKING AND SERVING THE OYSTERS

6. Make a bed of coarse salt on a baking sheet and place the filled oyster shells on it. Bake in the hot oven for 3-4 minutes.

7. To serve, place the oysters either in special oyster plates or on large dinner plates, bedded down in salt and without the upper shells.

Editor's note Samphire, a low-growing succulent sea-shore plant, can be occasionally found fresh at fishmongers, or can be gathered wild.

"Une recette pour apprendre à aimer les huîtres chaudes."

Tian de saint-jacques fraîches au beurre de champagne
Scallops with Champagne Butter

Preparation time: 2 hours
Oven temperature: 400°F/200°C/Gas 6

For four people

12 scallops, without their corals
4 ripe tomatoes, peeled, seeded and cut into fine strips
4 medium courgettes, finely sliced
1 clove garlic, finely chopped
1 teaspoon shredded basil
2 tablespoons olive oil
2 shallots, finely chopped
250 ml (scant half pint) champagne
180 g (6¼ oz) butter
a pinch of cayenne pepper
250 ml (scant half pint) whipping cream
salt, freshly ground pepper

"Plat typiquement niçois par son nom, remodelé à ma façon."

1. If the fishmonger has not already done so, remove the shells from the scallops, wash them and slice them horizontally into thick rounds. Set aside.

2. Preheat the oven. Have ready four metal tart moulds, open at the base, 4½" in diameter and ½" deep (see note). Arrange them on a buttered baking sheet. In each, put a layer of sliced courgettes, season with salt and pepper and place a layer of raw tomato on top. Sprinkle with chopped garlic and basil and season with salt and pepper. Press down firmly and moisten with olive oil. Cook in the oven for 20 minutes, covered with foil.

3. Sweat the chopped shallots with a little butter, moisten with the champagne and reduce the liquid by one quarter. Whisk 150 g (5¼ oz) of cold diced butter into this reduction over a very gentle heat. Season with cayenne, salt and black pepper. Strain the sauce and keep it hot.

4. Whip the cream until it is very firm.

5. Remove the baking sheet from the oven and mop up any juices with paper towels. Turn the oven to its highest setting.

FINISHING AND SERVING THE SCALLOPS
6. Arrange the slices of raw scallop in a beautiful rosette (as if you were making an apple tart) on top of each mould. Season with salt and pepper. When the oven is really hot, return the baking sheet and its moulds for 1 minute – not more. Then, remove the baking sheet and carefully lift off each mould with a large palette knife. Place the moulds on a cloth or a layer of paper towels to absorb excess juices, then put them on 4 heated flat plates. Keep hot.

7. Bring the sauce (3) to the boil and whisk the whipped cream in very rapidly with a small wire whisk.

8. Remove the metal circles and pour the champagne butter round the scallop moulds.

* You can improvise the moulds by stapling together lengths of stiff card covered with foil.

Fillet de loup aux lentilles vertes à la crème
Sea Bass with Green Lentils

Preparation time: 1½ hours

For four people

200 g (7 oz) small green lentils
1 shallot, finely chopped
1 carrot, peeled and diced
80 g (2¾ oz) butter
250 ml (scant ½ pint) dry white wine
1 or 2 fillets of sea bass weighing 600 g (1 lb 5 oz)
6-7 tablespoons whipping cream
2 tablespoons finely chopped parsley
2 tablespoons cognac
salt, freshly ground pepper

"Les lentilles, habituellement réservées aux traditionelles recettes de 'saucisses-lentilles' agrémenteront parfaitement ce plat de poisson."

PREPARING THE LENTILS
1. Soak the lentils for 1 hour in cold water. Drain, bring to the boil in fresh water and drain again.

2. Soften the shallot and carrot in a little butter and add the lentils. Moisten with the wine and an equal quantity of water. Season with a little salt and pepper, cover and cook gently for 40 minutes. Drain the lentils, keeping the liquid aside in a small pan.

PREPARING THE FISH
3. Cut the fish into four equal pieces. Season with salt and pepper and cook gently with the rest of the butter in a non-stick pan. Do not let it brown: the fish must remain white.

FINISHING THE LENTILS
4. While the fish is cooking, heat the lentils in a small pan with the cream. Bring to the boil and add the chopped parsley. Adjust the seasoning and divide the lentils between four heated soup plates. Arrange the cooked and drained fish on top and keep hot.

FINISHING AND SERVING THE FISH
5. Pour the fat from the pan in which the fish has cooked and deglaze with the cognac. Add the cooking liquid from the lentils (2) and reduce by half. Pour this sauce over the fish and serve immediately.

* Be careful not to use lentils which are too old or they will take much longer to cook.
* Turbot or other white fish can be used for this recipe.

Viennoise de loup à la purée d'aubergines
Sea Bass with Aubergine Purée

Preparation time: 1½ hours
Oven temperature: 450°F/230°C/Gas 8

For four
people

400 g (14 oz) sea bass, without skin or bones
500 g (1 lb 2 oz) aubergines
7 tablespoons olive oil
50 g (1¾ oz) butter
100 g (3½ oz) butter, clarified
100 g (3½ oz) white breadcrumbs (ideally from a day-old brioche)
juice of a lemon
2 teaspoons basil, chopped
salt, freshly ground pepper

"Une interprétation personnelle de 'l'escalope de veau viennoise'."

1. Cut the unpeeled aubergines into medium slices. Season them with salt and pepper and brush with olive oil, and fry briefly. Purée the aubergines, adding 2 tablespoons more olive oil. Pour into a small bowl and keep hot.

2. Preheat the oven to its highest setting or preheat the grill to its maximum heat. Have ready the warm clarified butter in one soup plate and the breadcrumbs in another. Cut the fish into 4 fine escalopes, and flatten them between sheets of plastic wrap, using a cleaver or a rolling pin. Season them with salt and pepper and dip first in the melted butter and then, on one side only, in the breadcrumbs.

3. Arrange the escalopes of bass in a roasting pan (breaded side up) and pour 4 tablespoons of water, 1 tablespoon of olive oil and the lemon juice round them. Scatter 50 g (1¾ oz) butter, diced over the top and place in the very hot oven or under the hot grill for a very short time – 2-4 minutes according to your equipment. The fish should be barely cooked through and an attractive golden colour.

4. Have ready four heated plates, and spread a layer of hot aubergine purée on each. Lift out and pat dry each escalope of bass and put one on each plate. Keep hot.

5. Strain the cooking juices from the roasting pan into a small saucepan. Bring to the boil and add the chopped basil. Pour this sauce round the escalopes and serve immediately.

* Breadcrumbs from a brioche are best for this recipe, but ordinary white breadcrumbs will do instead.
* Only a very little sauce is needed for this dish.

Loup demi-deuil
Sea Bass with Endives and Truffles

Preparation time: 30 minutes

For four people

1 or 2 fillets of sea bass weighing 600 g (1 lb 5 oz) skinned and boned
4 endives
40 g (1½ oz) preserved truffles *or* 1 small fresh truffle, brushed clean
200 g (7 oz) butter
1 tablespoon dry white vermouth
salt, freshly ground pepper

1. Cut the fish into four equal pieces. Cut the endives in julienne strips 1¼″ by ¼″. Slice the truffle finely.

2. Arrange these ingredients in a sauté pan – the order is not important. Season with salt and pepper and dot with the butter, add the vermouth and the same amount of water. Cover with foil and cook over a gentle heat for 15 minutes, turning the pieces of fish from time to time. Remove everything from the pan with a slotted spoon, leaving only the juice.

3. Arrange a bed of endive in each of four heated plates. Place a piece of fish on each and top with slices of truffle.

4. Bring the cooking juices to the boil, reduce to a light sauce, adjust the seasoning and pour over the fish.

Paupiette de raie aux poireaux et truffes
Skate with Leeks and Truffles

Preparation time: 1 hour

For two people
2 skinned and filleted wings of skate
2 leeks, trimmed and washed, white parts only
12 small new onions
2 tablespoons red wine vinegar
20 g (⅔ oz) truffles, sliced
150 g (5¼ oz) butter
1 tablespoon chopped chives
salt, freshly ground pepper

1. Season the skate with salt and pepper.

2. Cut the white part of the leeks into fine julienne strips. Peel the little onions and sweat them in a little of the butter with the leek julienne. Add 250 ml (scant ½ pint) water, salt and pepper and cook, covered, until all the liquid has evaporated, and the vegetables are glazed. Put them on one side, keeping the two kinds separate.

3. When the leeks are cool, spread them on the skate wings. Fold the wings over to form two "wallets". Put the stuffed skate in a sauté pan and add the glazed onions, the slices of truffle and the rest of the butter. Pour over the vinegar and 6-7 tablespoons of water, cover with foil and cook gently for 15 minutes, turning the skate after 7 minutes.

4. When the skate is cooked, arrange the pieces on two heated plates and sprinkle with the cooking juices. Decorate with the chopped chives just before serving.

* The skate "wallets" will keep their shape better if wrapped in plastic wrap before cooking. This film resists moist heat and can be used for all kinds of poaching and steaming.

"Un poisson qui peut subir presque toutes les sortes de cuisson: frit, poché, braisé, rôti, etc."

109

Ailes de raie aux cébettes
Skate with Little Onions

Preparation time: 40 minutes

For four people

200 g (7 oz) butter
40 small white new onions, trimmed and washed
4 wings of skate weighing 200 g (7 oz) each, skinned
1 tablespoon red wine vinegar
salt, pepper

For the parsley butter
50 g (1¾ oz) softened butter
2 tablespoons chopped parsley
juice of 1 lemon

1. Melt the butter in a large pan and add 500 ml (scant pint) water. Put in the onions, season with salt and pepper and cook, covered, for 40 minutes on a low heat.

2. Season the skate with salt and pepper and add to the onions in the pan. Pour in a wineglass of water and the wine vinegar, cover and simmer for 15 minutes.

3. Remove the skate and separate the flesh from the bony cartilage. Place the fish in a shallow serving dish and arrange the little onions on top. Keep warm.

4. Strain the cooking juices into a small pan and reduce by half.

5. Work the butter and parsley together to a paste, incorporating the lemon juice. Away from the heat, whisk the parsley butter into the reduced cooking juices. Check the seasoning and pour the sauce over the fish and onions.

Editor's note The parsley butter can be made in advance.

Grillade de saint-pierre à la vinaigrette au beurre
John Dory with a Sharp Butter Vinaigrette

Preparation time: 1½ hours
Oven temperature: 425°F/220°C/Gas 7

For four people

200 g (7 oz) best quality butter
4 medium waxy potatoes
1 new onion, finely chopped
4 fillets of John Dory weighing 150 g (5¼ oz) each *or* other white fish
4 tablespoons red wine vinegar
1 tablespoon chopped chives
salt, freshly ground pepper

1. Heat the butter until it is deep golden brown (beurre noisette) and strain it through a cloth into a bowl. Put on one side in a warm place so that any remaining solids can settle to the bottom of the bowl. Skim if necessary.

2. Cook the potatoes in their skins in salted water. Heat a ribbed grill pan or broiler and preheat the oven. Season the fillets of fish and sear them for a few seconds on each side to obtain an attractive diamond grid pattern. Remove to an oiled baking sheet and cook in the oven for 5 minutes.

3. Peel the potatoes and slice them finely while they are still hot. Divide them between four heated plates and place a fillet of fish on each.

4. Put 12 tablespoons of the tepid clarified butter (1) into a bowl with the wine vinegar. Whisk energetically until you have a smooth emulsion and season with salt and pepper.

5. Reheat the plates of fish and potatoes (3) for a few seconds in the hot oven, pour over the sauce and sprinkle each plate with very finely chopped raw onion and chopped chives.

* For the sauce to emulsify satisfactorily, the butter must be neither too hot nor too cold.

"Un plat très simple à réaliser qui reste léger et digeste, le beurre étant débarrassé de ses impurités."

La sole de "Loulou Bertho"
Sole "Loulou Bertho"

Preparation time: 25 minutes
Oven temperature: 450°F/230°C/Gas 8

For two
people

2 medium dover soles
150 ml (¼ pint) lemon juice
150 ml (¼ pint) olive oil
salt, pepper

1. Preheat the oven. The soles should be cleaned (if it has not already been done), but they should neither be washed nor skinned. They should be very fresh indeed.

2. Put both soles on a large sheet of foil on a baking sheet. Season them with salt and pepper and pour over the oil and lemon juice. Seal the edges of the foil to form a large container for the fish and their cooking liquid. Place the baking sheet in the hot oven and cook for 20 minutes.

3. When the fish are cooked, open the foil parcel and pour off the cooking liquid into a bowl. Peel back the skin of the soles and lift off the fillets. Arrange them in two deep heated plates, season with salt and pepper and pour over the cooking juices. Serve immediately.

* If you live by the sea, or are on holiday there, this is a marvellous way to cook soles straight from the sea.

"Loulou Bertho, haut personnage de la gastronomie azuréenne, installé depuis 26 ans à La Réserve du Cros de Cagnes, ami personnel à qui je rends hommage pour son savoir et ses connaissances sur le 'poisson du pays'; qui m'ont été très profitables."

Saumon frais au gros sel
Salmon with Coarse Salt

Preparation time: 2 hours

For four people

1 carrot, 1 cucumber, 1 turnip, 1 bulb of fennel and 1 celery heart, all peeled or trimmed and cut in 1″ sticks
1 courgette, unpeeled, cut in 1″ sticks
50 g (1¾ oz) french beans, trimmed
2 tomatoes, peeled, seeded and diced
250 ml (scant ½ pint) quality olive oil
a few sprigs of basil, chopped
500 g (18 oz) fresh salmon fillet, skinned
2-3 tablespoons coarse salt
salt, freshly ground pepper

1. Cook all the vegetables separately in boiling salted water until barely tender. Refresh each batch under cold running water and drain. Arrange in the upper part of a steamer or couscoussière.

2. Place the diced raw tomato in a large sauceboat or serving bowl and season with salt and pepper. Cover with olive oil, sprinkle with chopped basil and put in a warm place. (This sauce should be served tepid.)

3. Cut the salmon into four equal pieces. Season with salt and pepper and arrange with the vegetables in the steamer. Bring the water in the bottom half of the steamer to the boil and then put the top half in position. Cover and cook for 5-6 minutes, turning the salmon once.

4. Arrange the salmon and vegetables prettily on four heated plates alternating the colours of the different vegetables. Serve as soon as possible accompanied by a bowl of coarse salt and the tepid olive oil and tomato sauce. Each guest helps themself to sauce and salt according to their taste.

* It is vital to add the salt only at the last moment and it should be sprinkled evenly over the surface of the salmon.
* The choice of vegetables can be varied according to the season.

"Une variante du boeuf gros sel."

Filets de merlan "barigoule"
Whiting "Barigoule"

Preparation time: 1½ hours
Oven temperature: 450°F/230°C/Gas 8

For two
people

2 handsome whiting or other white fish
6 artichokes, purple for preference
1 tablespoon olive oil
1 onion, chopped
6-7 tablespoons dry white wine
1 lemon
2 fresh basil leaves
50 g (1¾ oz) butter
salt, freshly ground pepper

"Recette née de terre provençale et de mer azuréenne."

1. Remove the fillets from the whiting and pick out all the small bones, using tweezers. Skin each fillet. Butter a baking sheet and lay the fillets on it. Preheat the oven.

2. Remove the leaves and choke from the raw artichokes. Cut each heart into four pieces, keeping them in cold water acidulated with a little lemon juice to prevent them from discolouring.

3. Soften the chopped onion in the olive oil and then add the artichoke hearts. Season with salt and pepper and moisten with the wine and an equal amount of cold water. Cover and braise gently until tender. Drain, keeping the cooking liquid.

4. Purée the cooked artichokes and onion, and keep hot.

5. Sprinkle the cooking juices (3) over the whiting fillets and cook them in the hot oven for 4 minutes.

6. Divide the artichoke purée between two deep heated plates and place the fillets on top of the purée.

7. Bring the juices from the fish to the boil in a small pan, reduce well, add the juice of the lemon and season with salt and pepper. Pour this sauce over the fish and strew with a few shreds of fresh basil at the last moment.

* Soles, plaice and other flat fish can be treated in the same way.
* You can leave the cooked quartered artichokes whole, instead of making a purée.

Chartreuse de homard aux endives
Lobster with Endives

Preparation time: 3 hours
Oven temperature: 450°F/230°C/Gas 8

For four people

1 lobster weighing 800 g (1 lb 12 oz)
4 heads of endive
70 g (2½ oz) butter
juice of a lemon
1 carrot, 1 turnip, 1 cucumber, peeled and cut in matchsticks
50 g (1¾ oz) raw duck foie gras, diced
10 g (⅓ oz) truffles
2 teaspoons basil, chopped
250 ml (scant half pint) champagne
250 ml (scant half pint) whipping cream
salt, freshly ground pepper

1. Preheat the oven. Bring a large pan of boiling salted water to the boil and blanch the endives for a few minutes. Remove and drain them. Butter a sauté pan generously and put in the endive. Season with salt and pepper and lemon juice and add enough water to cover the endives. Cover with a circle of buttered greaseproof paper and a lid and cook in the oven for 1 hour.

2. Meanwhile cook the lobster for 20 minutes in boiling salted water. Remove the shell and keep hot.

3. Cook the carrots, turnips and cucumbers separately in boiling salted water, then refresh and drain them.

4. Separate the leaves of the cooked endives. Butter four metal moulds of the kind used for crème caramel and line the bottom and sides with the best endive leaves. Chop the rest coarsely. Cut the lobster meat into dice.

5. Melt the remaining butter in a large sauté pan and add the diced lobster flesh, and the cooked vegetables. Stir carefully, then add the diced foie gras and truffles, diced, the basil, salt and pepper. Moisten with the champagne and bring to the boil. Remove the various ingredients with a slotted spoon and pile them into a bowl. Keep hot. Reduce the champagne by one third, then add the cream and simmer until you have a thick sauce. Season with salt and pepper, strain and keep hot.

6. Stir 3 tablespoons of the sauce into the "fricassee" of lobster to bind it, and pack it into the lined moulds (4), pressing the contents down gently with the back of a fork. Finish with a layer of chopped cooked endive. Dot each mould with a knob of butter and return to the hot oven for 20 minutes.

7. Have ready 4 heated plates, and turn out a lobster "chartreuse" on each with the endive leaves on top. Mop up any juices which run out, using paper towels. Pour the hot sauce over each "chartreuse" and serve immediately.

* Good chicken or beef stock can be used instead of water to blanch the endives in step 1.

"Un gâteau moulé de homard aux légumes, avec une carapace d'endives."

Langouste rôtie injectée de sauce champagne à la seringue
Crawfish with Champagne Sauce

Preparation time: 30 minutes
Oven temperature: 450°F/230°C/Gas 8

For two people

1 crawfish
2 shallots, chopped
50 g (1¾ oz) butter
250 ml (scant half pint) dry champagne
250 ml (scant half pint) whipping cream
1 generous pinch of powdered saffron
6½ tablespoons olive oil
salt, freshly ground pepper

1. Preheat the oven. Soften the chopped shallots in the butter, moisten with the champagne and reduce the liquid by half. Add the cream and season with salt and pepper. Simmer for 5 minutes, stir in the saffron and strain into a clean pan.

2. Take up the sauce into a large syringe (*see note*). Place the crustacean on its back, with the tail well extended, and inject half the sauce through the "mouth" and the remainder through a hole made in the shell of the tail with a skewer.

3. Sprinkle the crawfish with olive oil and roast it for 20 minutes in the oven. Remove, cut in half lengthwise with a cleaver, and serve on two heated plates, with any juices which may run out when you divide it.

Editor's note Maître Maximin recommends a veterinary syringe for this operation, but a bulb-baster can be used instead.

"Rôtie avec sa sauce, serait-ce un précédent?"

Fricassée de homard aux pâtes fraîches
Fricassee of Lobster with Fresh Noodles

Preparation time: 1 hour

For four
people

1 lobster weighing 1 kg (2¼ lbs)
130 g (4½ oz) butter
2 shallots, chopped
1 teaspoon tomato purée
500 ml (scant pint) dry white wine
200 g (7 oz) fresh pasta (*see page 189*)
50 g (1¾ oz) raw duck foie gras, mashed
1 teaspoon tarragon, chopped
salt, freshly ground pepper

1. Kill the lobster and cook it for 20 minutes in boiling salted water. Remove the shell and pound the pieces in a mortar or with a rolling-pin. Keep the lobster meat hot.

2. Soften the chopped shallots in 30 g (1 oz) of the butter in a sauté pan. Add the tomato purée and then the pounded lobster shells. Moisten with the white wine and simmer until the liquid has reduced to about 250 ml (scant half pint). Strain into a small saucepan.

3. Cook the pasta in boiling salted water for 2-3 minutes. Drain and, in another sauté pan, mix in the mashed foie gras and a little pepper and heat gently. Divide between 4 heated soup plates. Slice up the lobster meat and arrange on top of the pasta. Keep hot.

4. Bring the reduced wine (2) to the boil, add the tarragon and whisk in 100 g (3½ oz) butter). Season with salt and pepper, skim, and pour this deliciously flavoured and coloured sauce over the lobster.

* You can replace expensive raw foie gras with the less expensive "mi-cuite" purée of foie gras.

Homard rôti "façon Loiseau"
Roast Lobster "Façon Loiseau"

Preparation time: 45 minutes
Oven temperature: 475°F/240°C/Gas 9

For four people

2 live lobsters weighing 1 kg (2¼ lb) each
300 g (10½ oz) Savoy cabbage
300 ml (½ pint) olive oil
50 g (2 oz) butter
juice of a lemon
salt, freshly ground pepper

1. Preheat the oven to its highest setting. Wash the cabbage and separate the leaves. Cook them in boiling salted water until they are still just crisp, then remove, refresh and drain.

2. Kill the lobsters and season with salt and pepper. Heat a roasting pan and pour in the olive oil. When it is very hot, put in the lobsters and roast for 10 minutes in the very hot oven. Then pour off the cooking oil and replace it with 1 litre (1¾ pints) hot water. Return to the oven and cook for a further 10 minutes. Remove the lobsters and keep hot, and strain the cooking liquid into a saucepan.

3. Cut the lobsters in half with a cleaver, crack the claws and remove all the flesh. Keep it hot. Crush the shells and add them to the cooking liquid (2). Reduce the liquid to 250 ml (scant half pint) and strain into a small saucepan.

4. Meanwhile, remove the tough stalks from the cabbage leaves (1). Slice the leaves finely into strips and toss them in the butter. Season with salt and pepper. Divide the cooked cabbage equally between four heated soup plates and arrange the lobster meat on top.

5. Adjust the seasoning of the broth (3) with pepper and a very little salt and add the lemon juice. Pour over the lobster and serve immediately.

* The lobsters can be replaced with langoustines.

"Bernard Loiseau: 'La Côte d'Or à Saulieu'. Il y a fort longtemps que 'l'aigle de Saulieu' est sorti du nid de la cuisine traditionnelle, aussi vu son talent et notre grande amitié, je me devais d'écrire sa recette."

Rizotto de homard safrané
Saffron Lobster Risotto

Preparation time: 1 hour
Oven temperature: 475°F/240°C/Gas 9

For four people

1 live lobster weighing 1.2 kg (2½ lb)
200 ml (⅓ pint) olive oil
1 onion, finely chopped
1 red and 1 green pepper, seeded and diced
2 large firm mushrooms, diced
1 fresh artichoke heart, sliced
200 g (7 oz) risotto rice
a pinch of powdered saffron
80 g (2¾ oz) butter
6½ tablespoons dry white wine
salt, freshly ground pepper

1. Preheat the oven to its highest setting. Heat 2 tablespoons of olive oil in a roasting pan. Season the lobster and roast it in the oil for 20 minutes, basting frequently.

2. Meanwhile, prepare the risotto. Heat the remaining olive oil in a medium sauté pan and add the vegetables, then the rice, salt and pepper. Let them cook very gently over a low heat, stirring, then add the saffron, 30 g (1 oz) butter, and enough water to cover the rice. Cook very gently until the rice is just tender stirring constantly and adding more water as necessary. It is very important that the rice is not allowed to dry out.

3. Remove the lobster from the oven and shell the claws and tail. Let them brown in the remaining butter in a separate pan. Meanwhile remove and purée the creamy parts and coral from the head.

4. Slice the meat of the tail into fine rounds and cut the claws in half. Keep hot. Add the wine to the butter in which the lobster meat has cooked, and bring to the boil. Reduce a little, then remove from the heat and stir in the lobster purée, season with salt and pepper and strain through a fine sieve.

5. Divide the risotto between four heated plates. Arrange the lobster meat on top, coat with the sauce and serve.

* Instead of the lobster purée, the sauce can be thickened with 100 g (3½ oz) of grated Italian mozzarella.

MEAT, POULTRY AND GAME

Tian d'agneau Niçois
Niçoise Lamb Fillets

Preparation time: 1½ hours
Oven temperature: 450°F/230°C/Gas 8

For four people
4 large ripe tomatoes
6½ tablespoons olive oil
1 onion, chopped
1 teaspoon chopped fresh basil
200 g (7 oz) button mushrooms
3 shallots, chopped
150 g (5¼ oz) butter
1 tablespoon chopped chives
500 g (1 lb 2 oz) spinach
2 lamb fillets, weighing 250 g (8¾ oz) each, trimmed
6½ tablespoons dry white wine
1 tablespoon truffle juice
1 clove of garlic
salt, freshly ground pepper

PREPARING THE VEGETABLES

1. Peel and seed the tomatoes. Chop them coarsely and sweat with the chopped onion in a tablespoon of oil in a small sauté pan. When the moisture has nearly all evaporated, season with salt and pepper, add the chopped basil and keep warm.

2. Wipe and trim the mushrooms, chop them finely and sauté in very hot oil until they give off their juices. Drain them and sauté them again with 1 chopped shallot and a nut of butter. Season with salt and pepper, add a tablespoon of chopped chives, drain once more and keep warm.

3. Remove the stalks from the spinach, wash it carefully and plunge into boiling salted water. As soon as the water returns to the boil, remove the spinach and refresh under cold running water. Drain and squeeze the leaves to remove excess moisture. Slice them finely and sweat them briefly in a little butter. Season with salt and pepper, drain and keep warm.

COOKING THE LAMB

4. Season the two pieces of lamb with salt and pepper. Fry them in butter for 3 minutes on each side so that they are still very rosy inside. Remove them to a deep dish to keep warm.

5. Pour off the cooking fat from the pan and add 2 chopped shallots and a nut of butter. Let the shallots soften, then add a teaspoon of the tomato mixture (1) followed by the white wine and truffle juice. Reduce by half, then add 250 ml (scant ½ pint) water, reduce by half and finally add the juices from the lamb. Season with a little salt and pepper and strain into a clean pan. Whisk in 50 g (1¾ oz) cold diced butter and keep hot.

ASSEMBLING THE DISH

6. For this you will need four open metal rings approximately six inches across and ¾" deep. The same result can be obtained by using stiff card strips covered with foil and stapled together. Preheat the oven.

7. Rub 4 plates with garlic and place a ring in the middle of each. Fill each ring with successive layers of spinach (3), mushrooms (2) and tomato (1), pressing each layer well down with the back of a fork. Each ring should be about ¾ full.

8. Carve the lamb into very fine slices and arrange the slices round the top of the circles as if you were making an apple tart. Season with salt and freshly ground pepper and heat through for 30 seconds in the hot oven. Remove the metal or card circles to reveal the layers of vegetables, and serve surrounded by the sauce (5).

* The meat must be very carefully trimmed with no trace of fat or sinew.

"Plat niçois par excellence, le tian est, à l'origine, constitué soit de sardines, soit de courgettes, de riz dressés en couches dans un plat en terre et cuits au four. Je lui ai donné une identité personnelle en réalisant les tians individuellement."

Persillade de noisettes d'agneau, sauce foies de volailles
Medallions of Lamb with Chicken-Liver Sauce

Preparation time: 1 hour

For four
people

2 fillets from a saddle of lamb weighing 350 g (12½ oz) each
100 g (3½ oz) beef marrow
1 teaspoon Dijon mustard
1 bunch of parsley, a clove of garlic, 2 sage leaves
3 shallots, finely chopped
3 tablespoons fine white breadcrumbs
150 g (5¼ oz) butter
2 chicken livers
750 ml (standard bottle) strong red wine
salt, freshly ground pepper

PRELIMINARY PREPARATIONS

1. Remove the membrane and fibres from the fillets of lamb. Season with salt and pepper and set aside. Reserve the trimmings.

MAKING THE STUFFING

2. Mince the beef marrow finely. Add the mustard, chopped parsley, garlic, one finely chopped shallot, the shredded sage leaves, breadcrumbs and a third of the butter. Season with salt and pepper mix well and set aside.

MAKING THE SAUCE

3. Sweat the two remaining chopped shallots in a little butter and add the chicken livers and a few of the lamb trimmings. Add a third of the wine and reduce very gently until it has almost all evaporated. Repeat with the same quantity of wine, then add the remaining wine and reduce to half its volume. Remove the lamb trimmings and sieve, pressing hard with the back of a spoon to extract all the juices. Bring to the boil, skim and whisk in 100 g (3½ oz) butter to bind the sauce. Season with salt and pepper and keep hot.

FINISHING AND SERVING THE MEDALLIONS

4. Cook the fillets of lamb in very hot butter for 2½ to 3 minutes so that they brown but remain rosy inside. Cut each fillet into six medallions, and arrange three on each of four hot plates. Cover each medallion with a layer of stuffing ½ inch thick and brown lightly under the grill. Wipe away any surplus fat from the plates and pour the chicken-liver sauce round the medallions.

* Serve with a "Jo's Gratin" (*page 201*).
* This dish can also be made with a best end of lamb.

Rognonnade de filet d'agneau
Fillet of Lamb with a Roulade of Kidneys

Preparation time: 2 hours

For four
people

1 aubergine
1 fillet weighing about 600 g (1 lb 5 oz) from a saddle of lamb including
    the "flap" and with the bones
6½ tablespoons olive oil
4 lambs' kidneys
4 tablespoons butter
1 small onion, chopped
2 tomatoes, peeled, seeded and diced
5 cloves of garlic
salt, freshly ground pepper

Editor's note This recipe produces a very rare result. If you like
your lamb a little less pink you will need to increase the cooking
time in stage 5 by a few minutes.

*"Un filet de selle d'agneau farci de rognon d'agneau, avec le moelleux de
l'aubergine et une pointe d'acidité due à la tomate, pour relever le tout."*

1. Cut the aubergine – unpeeled – into 10 thin lengthwise slices. Cook them briefly in hot olive oil on each side and drain on paper towels.

2. Skin the kidneys and season them with salt and pepper. Fry them in butter with a tablespoon of chopped onion until they are still just rosy on the inside. Remove and drain them.

3. Heat a tablespoon of olive oil in a small sauté pan. Add the remainder of the chopped onion, a crushed clove of garlic and then the diced tomato. Season with salt and pepper and cook until the mixture is almost dry. Allow to cool.

4. Spread out a rectangle of plastic wrap approximately 12″ by 8″ on the working surface. Lay the strips of aubergine (1) lengthwise, overlapping slightly. Spoon the reduced tomato mixture (3) over the aubergine slices with a palette knife. Season with salt and pepper. Arrange the 4 cooked kidneys (2) end to end horizontally across the aubergine slices and roll them up in the strips. Then roll up the plastic wrap to make a tight roulade shape. Twist the ends and place the "sausage" in the freezer for at least an hour to firm up the contents.

PREPARING THE FILLET

5. Trim the fillet of lamb and flatten the flap with a heavy cleaver. Season with salt and pepper. Remove the plastic wrap from the roulade (4) and lay the roulade carefully along the centre of the flattened fillet. Roll up the fillet and tie firmly in several places. Season and cook in a sauté pan with 1 tablespoon olive oil, a nut of butter, 4 unpeeled cloves of garlic and the chopped up bones from the saddle. Brown on both sides and cook over a medium heat for 10 minutes. It will be very rare (*see editor's note*). Remove the fillet to a sieve or wire rack over a dish to collect the juices.

FINISHING AND SERVING THE FILLET

6. Pour off excess fat from the sauté pan, keeping the garlic and bones. Deglaze with a wineglass of water and dissolve the caramelised juices. Reduce by half, add a second glass of water and season with salt and pepper. Reduce until you have about 6 tablespoons of juice. Whisk in 50 g (1¾ oz) cold diced butter away from the heat, strain and keep warm.

7. Remove the string from the fillet and cut in 12 slices which you then divide among 4 heated plates. Add the juices which have run out of the meat to the juice (6) and pour round the meat.

* Serve a Ratatouille "J.M." (*page 204*) with this dish.

Etuvée de langues d'agneau aux haricots rouges
Lambs' Tongues with Red Kidney Beans

Preparation time: 3 hours plus 12 hours soaking time

For four
people

8 lambs' tongues
200 g (7 oz) red kidney beans
a few drops lemon juice
4 large mild Spanish onions
100 g (4 oz) smoked streaky bacon
150 g (5¼ oz) butter
1 carrot
3 cloves garlic
bouquet garni made up of parsley, bay and thyme
750 ml (1¼ pints or one standard bottle) claret
1 tablespoon parsley, chopped
salt, freshly ground pepper

THE DAY BEFORE: SOAKING THE TONGUES AND BEANS
1. Place the tongues and beans to soak overnight in two separate bowls of cold water.

ON THE DAY
2. Place the tongues in a pan with enough water to cover and a few drops of lemon juice, bring to the boil and simmer for 10 minutes. Refresh under cold running water and drain. Using a sharp knife, peel the tongues and remove the tough coarse-grained parts and fat.

3. Drain the soaked beans. Peel the onions, leaving them whole, slice the carrot into large pieces and cut the bacon into little dice.

4. Heat 50 g (2 oz) butter in a heavy cast-iron pan and brown the diced bacon. Add the carrot, onions, garlic, the bouquet garni and the drained beans. Moisten with the bottle of red wine. Arrange the lambs' tongues on top of the beans, season with salt and pepper and cover with a sheet of foil and a lid. Bring to simmering point and cook very, very slowly for 2 hours. Open the pan and stir the contents carefully from time to time, checking to make sure that there is sufficient liquid. Add a wineglassful of water if necessary. Take care not to break up the onions as you stir.

5. Remove the onions from the pan and carefully hollow them

out with a spoon. Purée the contents of the onions and keep the purée and the hollowed-out onions in a warm place. Remove the tongues and set aside. Discard the carrots and the bouquet garni. Drain the beans, reserving the cooking liquid.

6. Put the drained cooked beans in a pan and stir in 100 g (3½ oz) butter and 1 tablespoon chopped parsley, over a gentle heat. Season with pepper and pile the beans into the four hollowed-out onions. Keep them hot. Reduce the cooking liquid by three quarters and slice the lambs' tongues finely.

ASSEMBLING THE DISH
7. Have ready four large heated plates. Put a stuffed onion in the middle of each and encircle with the hot onion purée. Arrange the tongue slices in a rosette round each onion and pour over the reduced cooking liquid (6).

* New season's beans are best for this dish.

"Un plat de ménage au goût du jour."

Filet mignon de veau en fondue
Veal Fondue

Preparation time: 1½ hours

For two people

4 medallions of veal, weighing 40 g (1½ oz) each
150 g (5¼ oz) butter
1 clove of garlic
200 ml (⅓ pint) dry white wine
50 g (1¾ oz) each of Emmenthal and Comté cheese, cubed
a few drops of kirsch
1 tablespoon flour
1 egg, beaten
50 g (1¾ oz) very fine breadcrumbs
1 shallot, chopped
1 teaspoon strong Dijon mustard
1 tablespoon chopped chives
salt, freshly ground pepper

PRELIMINARY PREPARATIONS

1. Season the medallions with salt and pepper. Heat 30 g (1 oz) butter in a sauté pan and cook the medallions until they are three-quarters done. Remove them, drain on paper towels and when they have cooled, put them to chill in the refrigerator.

MAKING THE FONDUE

2. Rub a small enamelled cast-iron saucepan or special fondue pan with garlic. Pour in half the white wine with some salt and pepper and bring to the boil. Add cheese to the boiling liquid, reduce the heat immediately and stir with a wooden spoon over a very low heat until the cheese has completely melted and you have a smooth mixture. Mix in the kirsch.

COATING THE MEDALLIONS

3. Take the chilled medallions of veal and plunge them in the melted cheese and remove them with a fork. Each piece will be coated with a layer of cheese which has solidified in contact with the cold meat. Roll them lightly in a little sieved flour, then dip in beaten egg and finally roll them in breadcrumbs. Set aside.

MAKING THE MUSTARD SAUCE

4. Soften the chopped shallot in a nut of butter, add the mustard and the remaining wine. Reduce by half and, away from the heat, whisk in 100 g (3½ oz) of cold diced butter. Season with salt and pepper, strain and keep hot.

FINISHING AND SERVING THE MEDALLIONS

5. Heat 30 g (1 oz) butter until it foams and fry the coated medallions (3) for 3-4 minutes on both sides. When they are golden brown drain them on paper towels and arrange them on a serving dish. Pour the mustard butter (4) round them and sprinkle with chopped chives.

* A galette of grated potato cooked in butter seems to me to be the ideal accompaniment for this dish.

"Des tournedos de veau 'transalpins'!"

Jarret de veau au potiron, sauce consommé
Shin of Veal with Pumpkin

Preparation time: 3 hours

For four people

4 slices of shin of veal, with the bone (as for ossobuco) weighing 300 g (10½ oz) each
1 carrot,
1 turnip
1 leek
1 stick of celery, cleaned and trimmed
1 onion, halved and browned
200 g (7 oz) pumpkin flesh
130 g (4½ oz) butter
a truffle weighing 40 g (1½ oz)
80 g (2¾ oz) vermicelli
1 egg, beaten
1 tablespoon chopped chervil
juice of 1 lemon
salt, freshly ground pepper

"Un ossobuco à la française."

PRELIMINARY PREPARATIONS

1. Cut the pumpkin into little sticks 1¼″ long by ⅛″ thick. Cook them with 30 g (1 oz) of butter, a little water and salt and pepper until they are still just crisp. Set aside.

2. Cut the truffle into fine julienne strips.

COOKING THE VEAL AND THE VERMICELLI

3. Fill a large earthenware stock pot with 4 litres (7 pints) cold water and add the vegetables and the shin of veal. Season with salt and pepper and cook very slowly, uncovered, for about 2 hours, skimming frequently.

4. When the meat has been cooking for about 1½ hours, ladle out 500 ml (scant pint) of the cooking liquid and bring it to the boil in a small saucepan. Cook the vermicelli in this stock and remove them to a colander with a slotted spoon. Reduce the stock in which they have cooked by three quarters.

MAKING THE PANCAKES

5. Put the vermicelli in a bowl and mix in the beaten egg and chopped chervil. Using either very small frying pans or individual tart moulds, form the mixture into four little pancakes or galettes and brown them on both sides. Drain them on paper towels and sprinkle with a little salt.

FINISHING AND SERVING THE VEAL

6. The meat will now be cooked. Continue cooking the stock but remove the slices of meat and place each one on a hot plate. Remove the central bones and fill the cavities with the cooked pumpkin sticks (2). Strew the truffle julienne round the meat and keep hot.

7. When the stock (4) has reduced to about half a pint (300 ml), add the lemon juice and whisk in 100 g (3½ oz) of cold diced butter. Check the seasoning and pour this sauce over the meat. Serve with the vermicelli "pancakes".

* Do not throw away any leftover cooking liquid. It can be used for other purposes or eaten as a simple bouillon with a little vermicelli or tapioca.

Poivrade de foie de veau aux endives
Peppered Calves' Liver with Endives

Preparation time: 1 hour

For four
people

4 medium heads of endive
4 shallots
190 g (6½ oz) softened butter
500 ml (scant pint) good dry white wine
20 g (⅔ oz) green peppercorns
1 bunch chives, finely snipped
4 slices of calves' liver, each weighing approximately 120 g (4½ oz)
6½ tablespoons sherry vinegar
4 fresh sage leaves
salt, freshly ground pepper

"*L'amertume de l'endive et la puissance du goût du poivre vert rehaussent le foie de veau, goûteux certes, mais ayant besoin d'un soutien de 'sauce condimentée'.*"

1. Remove the outer leaves of the endives and cut them in julienne strips 2″ long and ½″ wide.

2. Peel the shallots and chop them finely. Soften them in a heavy pan with a knob of butter, add 1 glass of white wine and reduce until the liquid has all but evaporated. Allow to cool, then mix in 100 g (3½ oz) softened butter and the green peppercorns. Season with salt and pepper. Push through a fine sieve and form into a sausage shape the width of a cork and 8″ long on a sheet of foil. Put to harden in the refrigerator or freezer.

3. Toss the strips of endive sprinkled with salt in 50 g (2 oz) butter, keeping them still crisp. Drain, and divide the endive between four heated plates large enough to spread them out. When the shallot butter has hardened, remove from the foil and roll in chopped endive (as if you were coating it with bread-crumbs). Cut the roll in 12 slices and return immediately to the refrigerator.

COOKING THE LIVER
4. Season the slices of liver with salt and pepper and cook them quickly in the remaining butter in a heavy frying pan. Drain off excess fat and place one slice on each of the 4 plates on which you have already arranged the endive. Keep hot in a warm oven.

COOKING THE ENDIVE AND SERVING THE DISH
5. Return the pan in which you have cooked the endive to the heat and pour in 250 ml (scant half pint) white wine and 6½ tablespoons sherry vinegar. Reduce until you have 4 tablespoons of liquid. Season with salt and pepper and strain over the slices of liver. Place 3 rounds of green pepper butter (2) on each slice. The butter will melt and impart its flavour to the meat and to the endive. Chop the sage leaves and scatter a little over each plate before serving.

* You should choose the very pale, just faintly rosy calves' liver which guarantees quality.

Crépinette de cervelle de veau "mousseline"
Potato Pancake Stuffed with Calves' Brains

Preparation time: 1 hour and 30 minutes

For four
people

500 g (1 lb 2 oz) potatoes
5 egg yolks
200 g (7 oz) butter
1 tablespoon double cream
2 sets of calves' brains
a few drops of lemon juice
a sheet of caul fat 16″ in diameter
2 large onions, finely sliced
1 litre (1¾ pints) beef consommé *or* stock made with a beef stock
    cube
1 tablespoon red wine vinegar
1 tablespoon sherry vinegar
salt, freshly ground pepper

* For the beef stock you can use either consommé or stock made with a stock cube.
* The onion purée must be very smooth indeed, with no unsightly fibres or lumps.
* A few capers can be added to the purée.

"Un soir d'hiver pour vous réchauffer le coeur."

PRELIMINARY PREPARATIONS

1. Peel the potatoes and cook them in salted water. Drain and purée them, adding the egg yolks, 100 g (3½ oz) butter and the cream. Check the seasoning and set aside.

2. Rinse the brains thoroughly under cold running water, taking care to remove all traces of blood and small veins. Put them in cold water with a pinch of salt and a few drops of lemon juice. Bring to the boil and simmer for about 15 minutes. Refresh under cold running water and drain. Cut them into fine slices.

COOKING THE PANCAKE

3. Lightly butter a 8″ frying pan. Lay the caul fat, first soaked for a few minutes in warm water and dried, in it, taking care not to tear it. Cover with a ¾″ layer of potato purée (1). Lay a rosette of slices of brain on top of the purée, cover with a second layer of purée and smooth with a palette knife. Turn in the overlapping edges of the caul fat so that the purée is completely enclosed. Put the pan over a moderate heat and cook for 15 minutes. When the underside is golden brown turn the "pancake" over very carefully and cook for a further 15 minutes.

MAKING THE ONION SAUCE

4. Meanwhile, make the onion and vinegar purée. Sweat the onions in 100 g (3½ oz) butter in a large shallow pan. Stir with a wooden spoon and when they have softened add the beef stock. Reduce over a gentle heat until half the liquid has evaporated and then purée. Strain through a fine sieve and add the vinegars. Taste for seasoning and keep hot.

FINISHING AND SERVING THE PANCAKE

5. When the pancake is ready, remove it from the pan and drain off excess fat with kitchen paper. Pick off any small unmelted pieces remaining from the caul, which should have melted completely. Serve immediately, handing the onion purée separately.

Ris de veau bardé de choux au sauternes
Veal Sweetbreads Wrapped in Cabbage Leaves with Sauternes

Preparation time: 2 hours
Oven temperature: 325°F/170°C/Gas 3

For four people

1 dark green savoy cabbage
4 veal sweetbreads weighing about 150 g (5 oz) each
1 carrot, finely chopped
2 shallots, finely chopped
50 g (2¼ oz) butter
350 ml (¾ pint) Sauternes or other sweet white wine
lemon juice
salt, freshly ground pepper

"De ris de veau 'bardés' de feuilles de chou que vous laisserez confire à four moyen."

1. Remove the leaves from the cabbage, cutting out the thick part of the stalks. Blanch them in boiling salted water, refresh under cold water, drain and set aside.

2. Rinse the sweetbreads thoroughly under cold running water. Put them in a pan with cold water, bring to the boil and simmer very gently for 15 minutes. Refresh and drain them. With a sharp knife, or your fingernails, remove the membranes surrounding the sweetbreads. Season with salt and pepper.

3. Soften the chopped carrot and shallots in the butter in a large sauté pan.

4. Preheat the oven. Spread out the blanched cabbage leaves (1) on a cloth and wrap up each sweetbread in one or more, so that it is completely enclosed. Arrange the four parcels on top of the softened vegetables in the sauté pan, pour over the Sauternes and cover with a sheet of foil and a lid. Bake for 1½ hours, checking from time to time that the liquid has not all evaporated. Baste the parcels with their cooking liquid from time to time and add a glass of water if necessary. Carefully remove the parcels in their cabbage wrappings, which will be very soft, and keep hot.

5. Strain the liquid remaining in the pan, spoon off all the fat from the top and reduce until you have about 8 tablespoons of thick syrupy sauce. Add a few drops of lemon juice and check the seasoning. Serve the parcels of sweetbreads either whole or sliced and surround with the sauce.

* It is most important that the parcels are very carefully made. They need not be tied up with thread, but you can seal them with plastic wrap, rolling them up so that the cabbage leaves are in close contact with the sweetbread.
* A "bouquet" of fresh vegetables (carrots, small turnips, and French beans) goes perfectly with this dish.

Rognon de veau rôti entier aux coquillettes
Roasted Veal Kidney with Fresh Noodles

Preparation time: 1 hour
Oven temperature: 450°F/230°C/Gas 8

For two
people

1 whole veal kidney with its fat
80 g (3 oz) small macaroni (coquillettes)
1 shallot, chopped
120 g (4 oz) butter
6½ tablespoons dry white wine
10 g (⅓ oz) truffles
1 tablespoon truffle juice
30 g (1 oz) cooked foie gras
salt, pepper

Editor's note It may be helpful to transfer the sauce to a double boiler once the liquids have evaporated.

"Un rognon qui garde tout son moelleux, rôti, dans sa graisse. En garniture, des coquillettes, mais quelles coquillettes."

1. Ask your butcher to remove all but a ¼″ layer of fat from a large veal kidney.

2. Preheat the oven. Season the kidney with salt and pepper and roast for 20 minutes, basting from time to time with its own melted fat.

3. Meanwhile, cook the pasta in boiling salted water until they are just "al dente", refresh them under cold water and drain. Sweat the chopped shallot with a knob of butter. Add the truffle juice and 2 tablespoons of white wine and reduce over a low heat until the liquids have all but evaporated. Keep the pan on a very low heat and whisk in 80 g (2¾ oz) butter, chilled and cut in dice. Season with salt and pepper. When the emulsion (beurre blanc) is ready and all the butter added, strain it through a fine sieve, pressing the shallots down firmly with the back of a spoon to extract all their juices. Keep the strained sauce hot.

4. Take the roasted kidney out of the oven and remove any excess fat on paper towels. Keep warm.

5. Heat the cooked pasta (3) with a knob of butter and season with pepper. Crush the cooked foie gras lightly with a fork and add to the pasta, together with the truffles, cut in tiny dice. Arrange in a serving dish.

6. Slice the kidney finely, seasoning each slice with salt and pepper and arrange on two heated plates. Pour any juice which may have run out of the kidney, into the hot sauce (3) and pour the sauce over the slices on each plate. Serve accompanied by the pasta.

Côtes de veau aux amandes
Veal Cutlets with Almonds

Preparation time: 20 minutes

For four people

4 veal cutlets weighing 130 g (4½ oz) each
2 tablespoons flour
1 whole egg and 1 yolk
1 tablespoon double cream or thick crème fraîche
150 g (5¼ oz) slivered almonds
100 g (3½ oz) butter
6½ tablespoons dry white wine
250 ml (scant half pint) whipping cream
salt, freshly ground pepper

PREPARING AND COOKING THE VEAL CUTLETS
1. Season the cutlets with salt and pepper and flour them lightly.

2. Mix the egg, the egg yolk and the double cream in a bowl. Dip the cutlets one by one into this mixture and then roll them in slivered almonds.

3. Melt the butter in a frying pan and cook the coated cutlets very gently for 4-5 minutes on each side. When they are done, remove them carefully and drain on paper towels. Keep hot.

FINISHING AND SERVING THE CUTLETS
4. Pour off the fat from the frying pan and deglaze with the white wine. When it has reduced by half, strain into a small saucepan. Add the whipping cream, salt and pepper and simmer until it has reduced by half.

5. Put each cutlet on a hot plate and surround with a good tablespoon of sauce. Serve with pasta or with a potato purée.

* The cooking in stage 3 must be *very gentle*, so that the almonds do not brown too much before the meat is cooked.

"Des côtes de veau panées d'une façon originale."

Daube de boeuf aux pieds de cochon et aux marrons
Daube of Beef and Chestnuts

Preparation time: 4 hours

For four to six people

1.2 kg (2 lb 10 oz) blade steak of beef trimmed and cut into cubes
100 g (3 ½ oz) lard
2 pigs' trotters, boned
500 g (18 oz) peeled chestnuts
250 g (8¾ oz) belly of pork
4 carrots, cleaned and cut into sticks
200 g (7 oz) little onions, peeled
4 cloves of garlic, peeled
50 g (2 oz) butter
1 sprig thyme, 2 sprigs parsley, 1 bayleaf
1 litre (1¾ pints) dry white wine
salt, freshly ground pepper

1. Season the beef with salt and pepper and brown in all but 1 tablespoon of the lard. Remove and drain. Cut the boned pigs' trotters into dice.

2. Slash the shells of the chestnuts and plunge them in boiling water for a minute or so. Peel with a knife, removing all the bitter inner skin. Cut the belly of pork into as many slices as you have chestnuts. Wrap each chestnut in a slice of pork and secure with a wooden toothpick.

3. Melt the butter and a tablespoon of lard in a heavy-bottomed cast-iron casserole. Brown the carrots and onions lightly then add the diced pigs' trotters, the herbs, the garlic, the browned beef (1) and the chestnuts. Stir until the ingredients are well browned and add the white wine. Season with salt and pepper, bring to simmering point and simmer gently, covered, for 3 hours.

4. Spoon off excess fat from the surface of the stew and remove the toothpicks from the chestnuts. Serve from the casserole, accompanied by potatoes boiled in their skins, peeled and rolled in melted butter and coarse salt.

* The cooking time will depend on the size of the cubes of beef and also on how tender it is.

"Il est bon de se retremper de temps à autre dans une cuisine bien rustique."

Rosaces de boeuf, sauce mode
Fillet of Beef with Wine Sauce

Preparation time: 3 hours

For four people 2 carrots, 1 split leek, 1 onion, 1 celery stalk, all cleaned and trimmed
1 calf's foot
4 good round carrots, sliced
50 g (2 oz) softened butter
150 g (5 oz) chilled butter, diced
50 g (2 oz) cooked foie gras
1 teaspoon cognac
1 bunch chives, snipped
1 large onion, peeled and finely chopped
750 ml (standard bottle) claret or other red wine
4 slices of fillet of beef, weighing 120 g (4 oz) each, trimmed
salt, freshly ground pepper, a few crystals of coarse salt

"Un fleur dans votre assiette."

1. Put the cleaned and trimmed vegetables in a large saucepan with the calf's foot. Season with salt and pepper and cover with cold water. Bring to the boil and simmer for 2 hours, skimming from time to time.

2. Remove the cooked calf's foot (1) from the pan and pick out all the bones. Cut the meat into small dice and keep warm.

3. Cook the sliced carrots briefly in boiling salted water, then refresh and drain them.

4. Mix the foie gras and the softened butter with a fork. Add a dash of cognac and season with salt and pepper. Form the mixture into a cylinder 6″ long and wrap in foil. Chill in the freezer. Chop the chives finely.

MAKING THE SAUCE
5. Soften the chopped onion in 1 tablespoon of butter, then moisten with a third of the red wine and reduce completely. Repeat with half the remaining wine and then pour in the rest and reduce to half its volume. Whisk in the cold diced butter. Season with salt and pepper, strain, pressing the onions firmly with a wooden spoon to extract all the juices. Keep hot.

PREPARING THE FILLET OF BEEF
6. Poach the slices of beef fillet for 10 minutes in the liquid in which the calf's foot has cooked. Cut each slice in two horizontally and arrange on four hot plates. Cover each slice with a rosette of carrots (3) as if you were making an apple tart. Sprinkle with coarse salt. Place some of the diced meat from the calf's foot around each slice of beef.

7. Remove the foie gras butter (4) from the freezer, roll it in chopped chives and cut into eight rounds. Heat the sauce (5), without letting it boil, if necessary.

8. Heat the beef through very briefly in a hot oven, pour the sauce over the meat and place a round of foie gras on each slide. The butter will melt and its flavours mingle with those of the sauce. Serve immediately with Garlic Croquettes (see page 211).

Os à la moelle farcis au plat de côte
Stuffed Marrow Bones

Preparation time: 3½ hours
Oven temperature: 450°F/230°C/Gas 8

For four people

500 g (1 lb 2 oz) top rib of beef
1 carrot, 1 onion, 1 turnip, 1 leek, 1 stick of celery, all peeled and trimmed
2 teaspoons black peppercorns
a bouquet garni of thyme, parsley and bayleaf
16 slices of marrow bone, ½″ thick
2 tablespoons parsley, chopped
1 tablespoon strong mustard
500 g (1 lb 2 oz) caul fat cut into 16 squares
1 tablespoon butter
4 shallots, chopped
salt, freshly ground pepper

* You can sprinkle the stuffed bones with grated Gruyère.
* Strips of belly of pork can be used instead of caul fat.

"Chauds ou froids, en été ou en hiver, d'agréables petits farcis simples à réaliser."

148

COOKING THE BEEF AND MARROW BONES

1. Place the piece of beef, the trimmed vegetables and the marrow bones in a large pan of cold salted water. Add the bouquet garni, the peppercorns and bring to the boil. Simmer for 2 hours, skimming carefully.

2. After 30 minutes remove the marrow bones with a slotted spoon and transfer the marrow to a bowl with a teaspoon. Rinse the empty bones under cold water, brushing them until they are perfectly clean.

MAKING THE STUFFING

3. When the beef is cooked remove it and the vegetables, reserving the cooking liquid. Mince meat and vegetables with the medium blade of the mincer or chop in a food processor. Add the mixture to the poached marrow together with the chopped parsley, mustard and 6½ tablespoons of the cooking liquid. Mix well, taste for seasoning and pack this stuffing into the cavities of the cleaned marrow bones. Wrap each in a square of caul fat, previously soaked for a few minutes in warm water.

ROASTING AND SERVING THE STUFFED MARROW BONES

4. Preheat the oven. Butter a gratin dish large enough to hold all the stuffed bones, and strew the bottom with chopped shallots. Arrange the marrow bones in the dish and moisten with 250 ml (scant half pint) of the strained cooking liquid. Cook for 30 minutes in the oven, basting frequently with the cooking liquid, adding more if necessary.

5. When the marrow bones are golden brown, drain them on paper towels and serve immediately accompanied only by a mixed salad.

Contre-Filet "canaille"
Beef Contre-filet with Steak Tartare

Preparation time: 30 minutes

For two people

2 pieces of contre-filet of beef weighing 200 g (7 oz) each
200 g (7 oz) rump steak, trimmed of all fat and sinew
½ onion
2 shallots
2 teaspoons capers
2 teaspoons chopped gherkins
1 teaspoon each chopped parsley, chervil and chives
2 very ripe tomatoes
1 teaspoon strong mustard
1 egg yolk
2 tablespoons olive oil
juice of 1 lemon
a few drops each of Worcestershire Sauce and Tabasco
30 g (1 oz) butter
1 tablespoon wine vinegar
salt, freshly ground pepper

"Moitié cru, moitié cuit pour les amateurs de viande et pour les déjeuners sympathiques entre amis."

1. This dish consists of a fried steak cut in two horizontally, stuffed with a layer of steak tartare and seasoned with a sharp tomato sauce. Mince the rump steak coarsely. Chop the onion, shallots, capers, gherkins and herbs separately.

2. Peel and seed the tomatoes, cut the flesh in small dice, and set aside.

3. Mix the mustard and egg yolk and then the olive oil in a bowl, then add the lemon juice, Worcestershire and Tabasco sauces. Season with salt and pepper and mix thoroughly with the chopped meat and the onions, shallots, gherkins and the herbs (1). Taste for seasoning and set aside in a cool place.

COOKING THE STEAKS
4. Cook the two pieces of contre-filet in hot butter until they are browned on the outside but still "saignant" inside. Keep hot. Pour off the cooking fat and deglaze the pan with wine vinegar. Reduce the liquid by half and add the diced tomato (2). Cook until the tomato is soft and the liquid has evaporated, and season with salt and pepper.

FINISHING AND SERVING THE STEAKS
5. Cut each steak in half horizontally, open them up and spread with the steak tartare (3). Close up the fillets so that you have 2 beef "sandwiches". Place them on 2 hot plates and cover with a layer of tomato (4). Serve immediately.

* This dish must definitely be served with potatoes baked either in the oven or in the ashes.

Noisettes de chevreuil au kaki
Medallions of Venison with Persimmon

Preparation time: 2½ hours

For two people 1 saddle of venison (roe deer) weighing about 600 g (1 lb 5 oz) before
  trimming
100 g (3½ oz) butter
1 carrot
3 shallots, finely chopped
1 tablespoon crushed black peppercorns
1 litre (1¾ pints) strong red wine
bouquet garni of thyme and bayleaf
5 cloves of garlic, crushed
100 g (3½ oz) fresh thin fettuccine noodles (*see page 189*)
30 g (1 oz) cooked foie gras
1 firm persimmon cut into 12 thin slices
1 tablespoon red wine vinegar
salt, freshly ground pepper

*"A la fois doux et acide, le kaki, un fruit idéal en accompagnement du gibier
pour un plat aigre-doux."*

PREPARING THE MEDALLIONS

1. Trim and bone the saddle of venison, or ask the butcher to do it for you. The trimmings and bones are important, so make certain they are not discarded. Break up the bones with a heavy cleaver. Cut the meat into six "noisettes" or medallions, and season with salt and pepper.

PREPARING THE VENISON STOCK

2. Brown the trimmings and broken bones in butter in a large sauté pan. When they have browned, pour off the fat and add the carrot, chopped shallots, crushed black pepper, bouquet garni and garlic. Moisten with the wine and bring slowly to the boil, skimming frequently. Simmer until the liquid has reduced to a half of its original volume. Strain and keep hot.

COOKING THE PASTA

3. Cook the fresh pasta in boiling salted water for 1-2 minutes. Drain and mix in the foie gras. Keep hot.

COOKING AND SERVING THE MEDALLIONS

4. Sauté the venison in very hot butter. The outside should be well browned and the inside still rosy. Arrange three medallions on each plate and surround them with the cooked pasta. Place two slices of persimmon on each noisette and keep hot.

5. Pour off the fat from the pan in which you have sautéed the venison, add the wine vinegar and let it evaporate. Pour in 500 ml (scant pint) of venison stock (2) and reduce till you have about 250 ml (scant half pint) of sauce. Whisk in 30 g (1 oz) butter in pieces, season with salt and pepper, pour over the medallions of venison and serve immediately.

* The venison stock is better made the night before.

Daube de lièvre au pain et chou rouge
Casserole of Hare with Red Cabbage

Preparation time: 3 hours
Oven temperature: 350°F/180°C/Gas 4

For six to
eight
people

1 handsome hare, weighing about 2.5 kg (5½ lbs) with its heart etc.,
　and blood
100 g (3 ½ oz) butter
6½ tablespoons olive oil
1 large red cabbage
1 kg (2¼ lbs) pork rinds
a bouquet garni, of thyme, bayleaf and a sprig of celery
black peppercorns
5 cloves of garlic
the zests of 1 orange and 1 lemon
1 sprig thyme
1 bayleaf
6½ tablespoons Cognac
750 ml (standard bottle) red wine, flamed to remove the alcohol
6 ends of two days-old French bread
1 whole onion
2 whole carrots, peeled
5 shallots, peeled
2 eating apples, preferably russets
coarse salt

PRELIMINARY PREPARATIONS

1. Make sure that you obtain the liver, heart, lungs and blood of the hare from your game supplier. Cut the hare into approximately 12 pieces and season with salt and pepper. Heat a large frying pan and melt 50 g (1¾ oz) of butter with olive oil. When the fat is smoking, brown the pieces of hare. When they have coloured, remove them immediately, drain and keep hot.

2. Separate the leaves of the red cabbage and blanch them briefly in boiling water. Refresh and drain.

3. Put the pork rinds in a heavy-bottomed pan with cold water to cover and a little salt, the bouquet garni and a few peppercorns. Bring to the boil and poach gently for 30 minutes. Drain and allow to cool. Slice into thin strips.

ASSEMBLING THE DAUBE

4. Have ready a large cast-iron casserole, with a lid, which will

fit into your oven. Preheat the oven. Line the bottom of the casserole with cabbage leaves (2) put in the pieces of hare (1) and then the sliced pork rinds (3), the garlic, orange and lemon zests, coarse salt, a few black peppercorns, a sprig of thyme, a bayleaf, the Cognac and the flamed red wine. Next add the bread, the carrots and the onion and finally the whole shallots. Cover and braise in the oven for 2 hours.

MAKING THE LIAISON FOR THE SAUCE
5. While the hare is cooking, purée the liver, lungs, heart and blood of the hare. Season with salt and pepper and keep aside. Peel and core the apples and cut them into 16 slices.

FINISHING AND SERVING THE DAUBE
6. When the meat is cooked, and the cabbage meltingly tender, remove the carrots, onion and herbs. Arrange the pieces of hare on a heated serving dish, surrounded by the cabbage leaves and the strips of pork rind. Purée the cooking juices, together with the stale bread, the garlic and the shallots, and strain this sauce, thickened by the bread, through a fine sieve. Heat the sauce gently and, away from the stove, stir in some of the purée (5) (*see note*). Check the seasoning, heat through for a second or two without boiling and strain on to the pieces of hare on the serving dish. Keep hot while you fry the slices of apple briefly in the remaining butter, drain and arrange them on the dish with the hare.

* Any sensible person will wonder why the already thickened sauce needs the addition of the liver purée. It is, in fact, very rich, and a tablespoon is enough to enhance the flavour of the sauce.

"Une daube liée au pain. Un élément de liaison trop souvent oublié si l'on veut utiliser de la farine coûte que coûte."

Lapin farci aux blettes et aux pignons
Rabbit stuffed with Chard and Pine Nuts

Preparation time: 3 hours
Oven temperature: 425°F/220°C/Gas 7

For eight to
ten people

1 rabbit weighing 2.5 kg (5½ lb)
fresh thyme leaves
1 teaspoon cognac
1 litre (1¾ pints) dry white wine
20 thin slices of fresh belly of pork
3 kg (6¾ lb) Swiss chard
100 g (3½ oz) butter
100 g (3½ oz) pine kernels, lightly toasted
50 g (1¾ oz) Smyrna raisins, soaked in warm water for 20-30 minutes
2 eggs
1 head of garlic
5 medium tomatoes, quartered
1 carrot
1 onion, finely chopped
1 bayleaf
500 g (1 lb 2 oz) rindless rashers of fat bacon
salt, freshly ground pepper

PREPARING THE RABBIT
1. Ask your supplier to bone the rabbit, making sure the bones are included with the meat. Spread out the boned rabbit, skin-side down, and season the inside with salt, pepper and a little fresh thyme. Sprinkle with the cognac and a little of the white wine. Cover the flesh with a layer of sliced belly of pork and set aside.

PREPARING THE STUFFING
2. Trim the Swiss chard, keeping the white stalks (ribs) for use in another recipe. Cook the green parts for 3-4 minutes in boiling salted water as you would spinach, then refresh under cold water, drain and squeeze to remove all excess water. Chop the chard and sweat with the butter in a large sauté pan.

3. Preheat the oven. Add the toasted pine-nuts, the pre-soaked raisins, a little garlic, salt and pepper. When the mixture begins to dry out, remove from the pan and set aside in a bowl to cool. Then, beat the eggs and add them to the mixture, stirring thoroughly. Form this stuffing into a large sausage shape and

156

place it on the boned rabbit (1). Fold the pork fat round the stuffing and then arrange the rabbit as near as possible to its original shape. Wrap the rabbit in bacon rashers and secure tightly with several lengths of thread.

COOKING THE RABBIT

4. Put the rabbit into a heavy earthenware or cast-iron oval casserole with the bones (1), the crushed cloves from a whole head of garlic, the white wine, the carrot, the tomatoes, the onion, a little fresh thyme and the bayleaf. Cover and cook in the oven for 1½ hours.

FINISHING AND SERVING THE RABBIT

5. When the rabbit is cooked, remove it carefully to a chopping board, catching as much of the cooking juice as you can as it drains. Reduce the liquid in the casserole until you have about 500 ml (scant pint). Strain through a fine sieve and remove the fat from the top, using paper towels. Correct the seasoning with salt and pepper and keep warm. Remove the threads and bacon rashers from the rabbit and slice it, arranging the slices on a warmed oval platter.

6. Add the juices which have run out of the rabbit to the reduced cooking liquid (5) together with the liver of the rabbit, if you have it, cut in small dice, so fine that they will cook through immediately. Serve in a sauceboat.

* A dish of fresh pasta with a basil sauce goes well with this dish.

"Un beau plat bourgeois pour une grande 'tablée'."

Gratiné de lapereau au girolles
Glazed Rabbit with Girolles

Preparation time: 1 hour

For four people 2 saddles of young rabbit, each weighing about 450 g (1 lb) on the
  bone
4 shallots, finely chopped
100 g (3½ oz) butter
a wineglass of dry white wine
400 g (14 oz) girolles (chanterelles) *or* other mushrooms
6½ tablespoons whipping cream
1 egg yolk
1 teaspoon red wine vinegar
1 tablespoon chopped chives
salt, freshly ground pepper

"A faire absolument en période d'automne, fin de l'été."

MAKING THE RABBIT STOCK

1. Remove the fillets from the saddles and trim off the silver membranes from the top. Chop the bones with a heavy cleaver and brown them in just over half the butter with a chopped shallot. When they are nicely browned, pour off the excess fat and deglaze the pan with a glass of white wine. Cook for 5 minutes and then add 8 tablespoons of water. Let this juice simmer until it has reduced by half, strain and set aside.

COOKING THE MUSHROOMS AND RABBIT

2. Clean the mushrooms and slice them finely. Cook briskly in half the remaining butter with the remaining three shallots. Drain and arrange the mixture as a shallow layer in the middle of a warm serving dish. Keep hot.

3. Cook the fillets of rabbit briefly in butter so that they are still faintly pink inside and slice them finely. Lay the slices, overlapping, on top of the mushrooms (2). Heat the grill.

FINISHING AND SERVING THE GLAZED RABBIT

4. Whip the cream till firm and add the egg yolk and a tablespoon of the rabbit juice (1). Coat each slice of rabbit with the mixture and glaze quickly under the grill.

5. Whisk in the remaining butter, in small cold dice, into the rabbit stock (1) with a teaspoon of wine vinegar and the chopped chives. Pour round the glazed rabbit and serve.

* You can use most wild mushrooms for this recipe, and, if there is no alternative, cultivated mushrooms.
* If you can't buy the saddles on their own, buy two whole rabbits and use the legs for a fricassee or a pâté.

Dos de lapin en feuilletage
Saddle of Rabbit in Puff Pastry

Preparation time: 1½ hours
Oven temperature: 475°F/240°C/Gas 9

For two
people

1 saddle of rabbit, boned, with bones and trimmings
the liver of the rabbit
3 shallots, chopped into tiny dice
1 small carrot, finely diced
1 courgette, finely diced but not peeled
200 g (7 oz) approximately of butter
500 ml (scant pint) dry white wine
A sheet of pork back fat
80-100 g (2½-3½ oz) fresh or frozen puff pastry
1 egg
Thyme; bayleaf, garlic
salt, freshly ground pepper

PREPARING THE STUFFING

1. Soften the diced carrot and one shallot in a little butter, without letting them brown. Add the diced courgette and let them sweat together for a minute or so before adding half the wine. Cover with a sheet of foil and a lid and braise very gently until the liquid has been completely absorbed.

2. Meanwhile liquidise the rabbit liver to a fine purée. When the vegetables are ready, remove the pan from the heat and stir in the liver purée with a wooden spatula. The heat of the vegetables will cook the liver instantly, binding the vegetable "stuffing". Add salt and pepper and set aside to cool.

STUFFING AND COOKING THE SADDLE

3. Beat the flaps that lie on either side of the saddle, which would otherwise contract during cooking and spoil the appearance. Season the meat with salt and pepper. Spread the "stuffing" (2) in a row of little sausage shapes down the middle and roll up the saddle, folding the flaps over to enclose the stuffing. Wrap it in a sheet of pork fat and tie up securely with thread.

4. Put the saddle in a sauté pan with the chopped bones and the remaining chopped shallots in a little butter and brown gently all over for about 15 minutes. Remove the saddle and allow to

cool. Pour off excess fat from the pan and deglaze with the rest of the wine. Reduce by half and then add 500 ml (scant pint) of water. Simmer until you have about 6½ tablespoons of juice. Strain and keep warm.

5. Preheat the oven to its highest setting. Untie the threads round the saddle and dry it with paper towels. Roll out the pastry very thinly. Beat the egg and brush the saddle lightly. Wrap the saddle up completely in pastry and seal the edges with beaten egg. Cook in the oven for 8 minutes, taking care the pastry does not burn or go too brown.

MAKING THE SAUCE

6. Meanwhile, bring the juice (4) to simmering point and whisk in 50 g (1¾ oz) of cold diced butter. Do not allow to boil. Season with salt and pepper and strain through a very fine sieve.

SERVING THE SADDLE

7. Carve the "saddle" into six slices and arrange three slices on each of two hot plates. Pour the sauce round the rabbit and serve.

* This dish can be accompanied by a Turnip Gratin (*page 209*).
* The rabbit's kidneys, if you have them, can be cooked to a rosy tenderness and added to the stuffing, thinly sliced.

"Un râble de lapin désossé farci d'une farce de légumes, enrobé de feuilletage."

Persillade de lapin de Garenne et ragoût de blettes aux raisins
Parslied Rabbit with a Ragoût of Swiss Chard and Grapes

Preparation time: 2 hours
Oven temperature: 400°F/200°C/Gas 6

For two people

The saddle and back legs of a wild rabbit in one piece
5 tablespoons olive oil
100 g (3½ oz) butter
250 g (9 oz) Swiss chard
lemon juice
1 tablespoon flour
1 bunch black or white grapes
100 g (3½ oz) fresh belly of pork cut in lardons
4 cloves of garlic
3 juniper berries
30 g (1 oz) chopped parsley
2 tablespoons fresh breadcrumbs
1 sprig thyme
1 tablespoon Dijon mustard
salt, freshly ground pepper

PRELIMINARY PREPARATIONS
1. Season the rabbit with salt and pepper and put in a roasting pan. Sprinkle with a little olive oil and a little melted butter. Put ready for the oven.

2. Remove the white ribs from the chard, keeping the green parts on one side. Peel the stalks with a potato peeler. Cut them into large julienne strips and put in a pan with cold water, a few drops of lemon juice, the flour and salt. Bring to the boil and blanch for a good five minutes, then drain.

MAKING THE RAGOUT
3. Preheat the oven. Peel and deseed the grapes.

4. Melt 50 g (1¾ oz) butter in a small enamelled cast-iron casserole and brown the lardons of belly of pork lightly. Add the chard stalks (2), 250 ml (scant half pint) water, salt and pepper. Cover and cook for 45 minutes on a low heat, checking from time to time to ensure that the liquid has not all evaporated, and adding a glass of water if necessary.

5. Meanwhile, make the persillade. Chop the garlic finely and add the juniper berries, crushed, the chopped parsley, thyme and the breadcrumbs.

ROASTING AND SERVING THE RABBIT AND GREEN CHARD PURÉE
6. Roast the rabbit (1) in the oven for 20 minutes, basting frequently.

7. While the rabbit is roasting, cook the green parts of the chard in boiling salted water, as if they were spinach. Refresh and drain. Squeeze to extract excess water and purée with 3 tablespoons olive oil. Heat this purée through, season with salt and pepper and keep hot.

8. When the rabbit is cooked, drain it on paper towels and paint it with Dijon mustard. Roll it in the persillade (5), sprinkle with the remaining butter, melted, and return to the oven to brown.

9. Cut the complete saddle in half lengthways. To serve, give each person a spoonful of green chard purée (7) in a neat oval shape and a piece of rabbit. Add the grapes to the ragoût of chard stalks (4) heat through and serve, still in the casserole in which it has cooked, at the same time as the rabbit. The juices of the ragoût provide the sauce for this dish.

* As a change you can use one of the varieties of flavoured mustards now obtainable.
* If you have started with a whole rabbit you can use the forelegs and ribs for a little stew or a Lapin chasseur with tomatoes and white wine.

"Un petit cul de lapereau sauvage rôti, moelleux à coeur et qui sent bon la Provence."

Cous de volaille farcis aux pieds d'agneau
Chicken Sausages Stuffed with Lamb's Feet and Wild Mushrooms

Preparation time: 4 hours

For four people

4 lambs' feet
juice of 1 lemon
1 tablespoon flour
1 carrot, scraped
1 onion, peeled
1 leek, trimmed and split
4 chicken necks, with the skin
1 bouquet garni
a few peppercorns
200 g (7 oz) butter
4 firm fresh cèpes (or other wild mushrooms)
2 chicken livers
1 tablespoon olive oil
3 shallots, chopped
2 eggs
1 tablespoon chopped chervil
salt, freshly ground pepper

PREPARING THE LAMBS' FEET

1. Place the lambs' feet in a large pan of cold water to which the juice of a lemon and a tablespoon of flour have been added and bring to the boil. When they have boiled for five minutes, refresh under cold water and drain.

2. Put the drained lambs' feet in a large pan with the carrot, onion, leek, bouquet garni, salt and a few whole peppercorns and cover with cold water. Bring to the boil and simmer gently for 2 hours, skimming frequently.

PREPARING AND STUFFING THE CHICKEN NECKS

3. Meanwhile, remove the skins from the chicken necks without tearing, so that they make four tubes which will be used as sausage skins. Soak the skins under cold running water for 30 minutes. Chop the necks and brown them lightly in butter. Pour off the fat and add the stalks of the cèpes, chopped finely. Cover with 1 litre (1¾ pints) cold water. Bring to the boil and simmer until reduced to a quarter. Strain and reserve this "cèpe juice".

4. Clean and slice the heads of the cèpes and fry them briskly in a mixture of butter and olive oil. Drain and set aside.

5. Fry the chicken livers briefly in 30 g (1 oz) butter together with the chopped shallots. The livers should remain rosy inside. Drain, and rub through a sieve or liquidise. Add the fried cèpes, eggs and chervil, season with salt and pepper and set aside.

6. When the lambs' feet (2) are cooked, lift them out with a slotted spoon and remove the skin and all the bones and pieces of gristle. Cut the meat in small dice add to the cèpes and chicken liver stuffing. Chill in the refrigerator. Keep the liquid in which the lambs' feet have cooked.

7. Drain the chicken neck-skins and dry them, removing the sinews and any traces of fat (turn them inside out to do this). Tie each skin at one end with string and pack in the chilled filling to make 4 sausages of equal size. Tie the open ends with thread and simmer for 1½ hours in the liquid in which the lambs' feet have cooked, skimming carefully. When they are cooked, remove and drain them, patting them dry with paper towels. Allow to cool.

FINISHING AND SERVING THE SAUSAGES
8. When they are cold, prick the cooled "sausages" with a needle and fry them in butter until they are nicely browned all over. Bring the cèpe juice (3) to the boil and whisk in 100 g (3½ oz) diced cold butter. Season with salt and pepper. Remove excess fat from the "sausages" with kitchen paper and serve with the cèpe sauce and a potato gratin (*see page 201*).

* To prevent the "sausages" bursting while they are poaching, seal each one in plastic wrap.

"A vous faire attraper la chair de poule tellement c'est bon."

Poulet rôti, beurre de noix
Roast Chicken with Walnut Butter

Preparation time: 1½ hours
Oven temperature: 450°F/230°C/Gas 8

For four people

1 large free-range chicken weighing 1.8 kg (4 lbs)
200 g (7 oz) butter
100 g (3 oz) walnut kernels, skinned
1 tablespoon strong mustard
1 teaspoon cognac
2 teaspoons oil
8 medium potatoes, peeled and sliced
salt, freshly ground pepper

"Pour les amateurs d'une cuisine rustique."

1. Prepare the chicken for cooking if this has not already been done. The skin should be unbroken.

2. Crush the walnuts and mix thoroughly with the butter, mustard, cognac, and a little salt and pepper.

3. Preheat the oven. Use your fingers or a rounded knife to separate the skin of the chicken from its flesh, taking care not to tear it. Push in the walnut butter under the skin and massage the bird so that the butter is well distributed over the flesh. Truss and season the chicken and brush it with a little oil. Place in a lightly oiled roasting pan with the sliced potatoes and cook in the hot oven for approximately 50 minutes. As the walnut butter melts it will permeate first the flesh of the chicken and then the potatoes, which will become golden, moist and flavoured to perfection.

4. To serve, cut the chicken in four pieces, removing as many bones as possible. No sauce is needed.

* It is essential to have a genuine farm bird for this dish. A French cook would look for one from the Tarn or from Bresse.

Galette de pigeonneau, sauce tapioca
Delicate Pigeon Pie

Preparation time: 2 hours
Oven temperature:

*For four
people* 4 young pigeons weighing 300 g (10½ oz) each
1 kg (2¼ lbs) fresh green almonds
500 g (18 oz) chanterelles
4 tablespoons olive oil
200 g (7 oz) flaky pastry dough, fresh or frozen
1 shallot, chopped
200 g (7 oz) butter
1 egg, beaten
25 g (1 oz) tapioca
salt, freshly ground pepper

PRELIMINARY PREPARATIONS

1. Clean and singe the birds if it has not already been done. Remove and skin the breasts and legs and reserve the carcasses.

2. Shell the fresh almonds and split them in two, removing the outer skin.

3. Clean and slice the chanterelles. Brown them in hot oil until they have given off their moisture. Drain and press them gently, and set aside.

4. Roll out the pastry in two circles 10″ and 12″ in diameter and keep in a cold place.

5. Sauté the chanterelles (3) in butter with the chopped shallot and a little salt and pepper. Drain and allow to cool completely.

6. Season the breasts with salt and pepper and cook them in hot butter, for 1½ minutes. They should be very rare. Drain on paper towels and cut into narrow strips.

PREPARING THE PIE

7. Spread the smaller of the two pastry circles (4) on a moistened baking sheet and cover it with a layer of chanterelles (5) then the strips of pigeon, a second layer of chanterelles and finally, the almonds (2). Moisten the edges of the pastry with water and cover with the second, larger circle, sealing the edges firmly. Make an opening ¾″ across in the top, brush with beaten

168

egg and score with a fork to make an attractive grille pattern. Set aside in the refrigerator while you make the sauce.

MAKING THE SAUCE

8. Break up the bones of the birds with a cleaver and put them to brown in a little butter. Pour off the excess fat and moisten the browned carcasses with 500 ml (scant pint) of water. Bring to the boil, simmer for half an hour and strain the liquid into a medium-sized saucepan, discarding the bones. Bring to the boil and drop in the tapioca in a fine rain. Let it poach gently for a few minutes. Preheat the oven to its highest setting.

9. When the tapioca is cooked, remove it with a slotted spoon and keep warm. Reduce the liquid in which it has cooked to half and, away from the heat, whisk in 100 g (3½ oz) of cold diced butter. Check the seasoning and keep hot.

COOKING AND SERVING THE PIE

10. When the oven is really hot, put in the galette (7) and bake for 8 minutes (a little longer if necessary but watch that the pastry does not burn).

11. Meanwhile, season the legs with salt and pepper and fry them in butter, for three to four minutes.

12. Return the poached tapioca to the sauce (9). Cut the cooked pie into 4 and arrange on 4 hot plates with two legs to each plate and pour the sauce round the side.

* The sauce can be poured into the galette through the opening in the middle after it has cooked, and just before serving, but you will run the risk of ending up with soggy pastry.

* Dried or fresh cèpes can be used instead of chanterelles.
* This is a version of a North African dish which uses filo pastry.

Filets de pigeon en ravioli, sauce hachée
Pigeon Ravioli

Preparation time: 3 hours

For four people

2 plump pigeons weighing 500 g (18 oz) each (with their giblets)
150 g (5 oz) butter
2 large or 4 small thin slices of Parma ham (prosciutto)
2 shallots, chopped
6½ tablespoons dry white wine
250 ml (scant ½ pint) port
200 g (7 oz) pasta dough (*see page 189*)
1 onion, chopped
1 tablespoon olive oil
2 tomatoes, peeled, seeded and cut into dice
a few leaves of fresh sage, chopped
salt, freshly ground pepper

PRELIMINARY PREPARATIONS
1. Skin the birds and lift off the breasts. Remove the legs and bone them. Chop the leg meat very finely with the livers and gizzards and set aside. Chop up the carcasses with a cleaver.

2. Season the breast fillets with salt and pepper and cook them in hot butter. Do no overcook them: they should still be rosy inside. Drain them on kitchen paper. When they have cooled, wrap each fillet in a piece of Parma ham. Then roll up each fillet in plastic wrap to make four firm little sausages. Put them in the freezer to stiffen.

3. Brown the carcasses in butter with 2 chopped shallots. Pour off the excess fat and moisten with the white wine. Let it evaporate completely and pour in the port and 250 ml (scant ½ pint) water. Simmer over a low heat until the liquid has reduced by half. Strain and discard the bones.

MAKING THE RAVIOLI
4. Roll out the pasta dough as thinly as possible. Cut out 1½" circles.

5. Remove the "sausages" from the freezer, unwrap them and cut them into ⅛" slices. Put one slice on half the circles of pasta dough, moisten the edges with a little water and cover with a second circle, sealing the edges well with your thumb. Put the ravioli on a tray in the refrigerator.

MAKING THE SAUCE

6. Sweat the chopped onion in 30 g (1 oz) butter and 1 table-spoon of olive oil in a small saucepan. When the onion has softened, add the chopped raw pigeon (1), stir briefly and add the chopped tomato. Pour in the stock (3), season and simmer until you have a fairly thick sauce.

FINISHING AND SERVING THE RAVIOLI

7. Bring a pan of salted water to the boil and poach the ravioli for 7-8 minutes. Spoon the sauce (6) on to 4 hot plates and arrange the drained cooked ravioli on top. Sprinkle with a little chopped fresh sage.

* In this recipe it is very important that the pigeon breasts are not overcooked.

"Des filets de pigeon en 'croûte' moelleuse sur une sauce façon bolognaise."

Pigeons en gouttière
Hot Pigeon Terrine

Preparation time: 3 hours
Oven temperature: 475°F/240°C/Gas 9

*For six
people*

3 large pigeons weighing 500 g (18 oz) each
2 carrots sliced
2 turnips sliced
2 courgettes, peeled and cut into thin slices
250 ml (scant ½ pint) oil
2 red peppers
50 g (1¾ oz) lean veal, chilled
6½ tablespoons whipping cream
180 g (6½ oz) butter
2 shallots, chopped
6½ tablespoons each of dry white wine and port
salt, freshly ground pepper

Note: For this recipe you must have a cylindrical hinged metal mould of the kind used for making *pain de mie* or round sandwich loaves, at least 4″ in diameter. When it is open, each half looks like a section of rainwater guttering closed off at each end. Only one half is used for the recipe: the other half can be weighted down with water or pebbles if necessary.

PRELIMINARY PREPARATIONS

1. Cook the sliced carrots, turnips and courgettes separately in boiling salted water. Refresh and drain them.

2. Heat the oil until it smokes and fry the peppers for about 2 minutes. Drain them, and when they are tepid peel them and cut them in strips, discarding the seeds.

3. Clean and singe the birds if they have not already been prepared. Remove and skin the breast fillets and the legs and chop the carcasses with a cleaver.

4. Purée the cold veal and add the whipping cream and continue until you have a smooth purée. Season with salt and pepper and keep cold in the refrigerator.

5. Season the breast fillets with salt and pepper. Fry them briefly in butter – they should remain rare inside – drain them on paper towels and allow them to cool.

PREPARING AND COOKING THE TERRINE

6. Preheat the oven to its hottest setting. Butter one half of the mould lavishly and line it with successive layers of peppers, courgettes, carrots and turnips. Trim off any pieces which protrude over the edge of the mould. By this time the "gutter" will be half full. Fill the remaining space with the veal purée (4), placing the cooked pigeon fillets (5) in the middle of the layer of purée. Press down lightly with a spatula, and smooth the top. Cover with buttered paper and cook in a bain-marie or a roasting tin containing water for 45 minutes in the oven.

PREPARING THE STOCK

7. While the terrine is cooking, prepare the sauce. Brown the carcasses (1) in butter with 2 chopped shallots. Pour off the fat and deglaze with the white wine and port. Let the liquid evaporate and pour in enough cold water to cover the bones. Simmer until the liquid has reduced to three quarters.

FINISHING AND SERVING THE TERRINE

8. When the pigeon terrine is cooked, turn it, gutter and all, over on to a tray. Let it rest for at least 15 minutes while the juices run out and meanwhile cook the seasoned pigeon legs in butter. Add 100 g (3½ oz) butter in dice to the boiling stock (7), then season with salt and pepper and strain. Ease off the mould from the terrine and slice it into 12 even slices. Place two on each hot plate, arranging them flat sides together to form a circle, place a cooked leg on each circle and surround with the sauce.

* Turnips, braised endive or Brussels sprouts can all be used as a vegetable garnish, or you could serve fresh pasta.
* Leave time for the terrine to drain and solidify before you attempt to unmould and slice it.

"Une terrine de pigeon chaude avec un montage original."

Brochette de canard aux olives
Skewered Duck with Olives

Preparation time: 1 hour

*For four
people*

2 duck breasts, raw and with their skin
8 medium cèpes
8 slices of belly of pork
1 whole head of garlic
6½ tablespoons olive oil
100 g (3½ oz) stoned green olives
150 g (5 oz) butter
lemon juice
1 red pepper
1 green pepper
2 raw duck livers
1 onion, chopped
150 g (5 oz) risotto rice
250 ml (scant ½ pint) chicken stock
salt, freshly ground pepper

PREPARING THE BROCHETTES

1. Cut the magrets into 1″ cubes, retaining the skin. Clean the cèpes and cut them into cubes of the same size and do the same with the belly of pork.

2. Run four skewers through the head of garlic to flavour the metal. Then arrange the duck, cèpes and belly of pork alternately, taking care that the skin side of the duck always faces the same way. Season each brochette with salt and pepper and sprinkle with a little olive oil.

PREPARING THE OLIVE BUTTER

3. Blanch the olives in a big pan of boiling water for approximately 10 minutes. Refresh under cold water and drain in a colander. Then purée with 100 g (3½ oz) butter, a squeeze of lemon juice, salt and pepper. Spread the olive butter in a thin layer on a flat plate and chill. Then divide into squares the same size as the pieces of duck.

4. Cut the unpeeled peppers and the duck livers into small dice and sauté them separately in very hot oil for a few seconds. Drain and set aside.

COOKING THE RICE

5. Melt 50 g (2 oz) of butter in a medium sauté pan and soften the chopped onion, then add the rice. Stir the mixture round so that the butter coats the rice and pour in enough chicken stock to cover. Cook on a low heat, stirring from time to time with a wooden spoon and adding more stock if necessary. After 15-20 minutes the rice should be swollen and perfectly cooked. Add the cubes of peppers and duck liver (4) and 50 g (1¾ oz) butter and keep hot.

6. Grill the brochettes in the usual way, giving the skin side a little extra time as the skin must be well done.

7. Divide the risotto (5) between four heated plates and place a skewer on each. At the last moment, put a square of olive butter (3) on top of each piece of duck breast.

* If you can get some duck hearts they can be skewered between the cèpes and the pieces of duck breast.

"Une brochette franco-italienne. . . ."

Crépinettes de filet de canard aux huîtres
Duck Breast with Oysters

Preparation time: 2 hours

For four people

2 duck breasts
12 oysters
200 g (7 oz) butter
3 shallots, finely chopped
1 carrot, finely diced
250 ml (scant ½ pint) dry white wine
2 duck gizzards
2 duck livers
a sheet of pork caul fat
250 ml (scant ½ pint) red Bordeaux wine
30 g (1 oz) raw duck foie gras
salt, freshly ground pepper

PRELIMINARY PREPARATIONS

1. Remove the skin from the two duck breasts (magrets) and season them with salt and pepper.

2. Open the oysters and poach them, starting with cold water and removing them just before the water begins to boil. Keep warm.

MAKING THE DUCK'S LIVER PARCELS

3. Melt 50 g (1¾ oz) butter in a sauté pan, add the diced carrot and two chopped shallots, stir and pour in the white wine. Cover with greaseproof paper or foil and cook until the liquid is completely evaporated.

4. Mince the gizzards (carefully cleaned) and the livers very finely or chop them in a food processor and mix with the vegetables in the sauté pan (3). Stir and season with salt and pepper.

5. Cut the caul fat into twelve squares. Wet your hands and form the liver and vegetable mixture (4) into little balls. Wrap each one in caul fat, flatten each little parcel slightly with the palm of your hand and set aside.

COOKING THE DUCK BREASTS

6. Heat 50 g (1¾ oz) butter until it sizzles and cook the magrets for 4 minutes. They should still be rosy inside. When they are done let them rest in a warm place. Pour off the fat from the pan and soften the remaining chopped shallot with a nut of butter. Pour in the red wine and reduce over a gentle heat.

FINISHING AND SERVING THE DUCK BREAST PARCELS

7. Meanwhile, fry the duck's liver parcels in butter for 3-4 minutes on each side. Season with salt and pepper.

8. Purée the foie gras. When the sauce (6) has reduced by half, remove the pan from the heat and whisk in 100 g (3½ oz) cold diced butter and then the raw foie gras reduced to a purée. Check the seasoning and strain through a fine sieve or a wet muslin into a clean pan. Keep hot on the edge of the stove or in a bain-marie, but do not boil.

9. Slice the duck breasts into 12 thick slices. Arrange 3 little parcels on each of four hot plates. Place a piece of duck breast surmounted by an oyster on each parcel. Give each plateful a turn of the peppermill and heat through very briefly in a hot oven. Pour over the hot sauce (8) and serve immediately.

* A fresh spinach purée goes very well with this dish.

"Un mélange audacieux mais parfaitement réussi."

Canard rôti à l'ail
Roast Duck with Garlic

Preparation time: 1 hour
Oven temperature: 450°F/230°C/Gas 8

For four
people

1 Barbary duck of approximately 2 kg (4½ lbs)
20 cloves of garlic
250 g (8¾ oz) butter
100 g (3½ oz) parsley
1 teaspoon strong Dijon mustard
2 tablespoons olive oil
4 heads of endive
250 ml (scant ½ pint) dry white wine
salt, freshly ground pepper

PREPARING THE ENDIVES
1. Cut the endives into julienne strips. Season the duck liver with salt and pepper and fry it briefly keeping it pink inside. Drain it.

PREPARING THE DUCK
2. Clean and singe the Barbary duck if it has not already been prepared. Reserve the neck and wingtips. Preheat the oven.

3. Peel and flatten the cloves of garlic and put them in a bowl with 100 g (3½ oz) butter, the parsley sprigs, mustard, salt and pepper. Mix everything together and stuff the duck with it. Truss securely with string, and season the outside with salt and pepper. Roast in the hot oven for 18 minutes, basting with a little olive oil.

4. When the duck is cooked, place it on a board. Remove the breast fillets and the legs. Keep the breast fillets warm, and, after cutting through the leg joints, cook the legs in a little butter.

5. Remove the cloves of garlic and parsley from the inside of the duck. Chop up the carcass and trimmings in the remaining juices. Deglaze the pan with a glass of white wine and reduce. Then add enough water to cover the bones and reduce until you have 200 ml (⅓ pint) liquid. Strain and keep hot.

FINISHING THE ENDIVES

6. Fry the strips of endive in butter with salt and pepper. When they have softened remove and drain them. Mash the cooked duck liver (1) with a fork and mix with the endives. Divide this mixture between four hot plates.

FINISHING AND SERVING THE DUCK

7. Cut the two duck fillets into thin strips and arrange them in an overlapping pattern on top of the endives. Divide each leg in two and put one piece on each plate. Pepper the duck strips. Bring the sauce (5) to the boil and, away from the heat, whisk in 100 g (3½ oz) cold diced butter. Taste for seasoning and pour over the duck fillets.

* Choose a female duckling if possible. They are always tenderer.
* If you find that the strips of duck breast are too underdone, put the plates back into the hot oven for a moment.

Editor's note To many people, a duck cooked as briefly as this would definitely be too raw – add an extra ten minutes if you like your duck just pink. This dish can be served decorated with whole peeled and cooked cloves of garlic.

"Un canard bourré d'ail, dont seul le parfum subsiste."

Sarcelle aux poires rôties
Wild Duck with Pears

Preparation time: 2 hours plus 24 hours
Oven temperature: 475°F/240°C/Gas 9.

For two people
1 wild duck – preferably a teal, and hung for 3-4 days
2 very ripe pears
500 ml (scant pint) red wine
1 pinch cinnamon
1 carrot, cleaned and cut in pieces
1 onion, peeled and cut in pieces
1 tablespoon olive oil
120 g (4¼ oz) butter
2 crushed, unpeeled garlic cloves
1 vanilla pod, split in two
salt, freshly ground pepper

For the Salad
A handful of lamb's lettuce
4 teaspoons vinaigrette

PRELIMINARY PREPARATIONS
The Day Before
1. Peel the pears, cut them in half and marinate in the red wine with the pinch of cinnamon.

On the Day
2. Pluck and clean the wild duck if it has not already been done. Salt the bird inside and out and truss with fine string. Chop the neck, wing tips and other trimmings. Preheat the oven to its hottest setting.

3. Remove the pears from their marinade with a slotted spoon and dry them. Reserve the marinade.

ROASTING THE DUCK
4. Put the duck in a roasting tin and sprinkle with olive oil. Add 70 g (2½ oz) butter, the crushed trimmings, the cloves of garlic and the onion and carrot. Roast for 12 minutes, basting frequently.

5. Remove the duck and keep warm. Keep the trimmings and the vegetables in the roasting pan and pour off the excess fat. Moisten with the marinade (3). Reduce over a good heat until you have approximately 6 tablespoons of sauce.

6. Meanwhile, turn the oven down one point, and roast the pears with a little butter, salt, and a little pepper for 5-6 minutes.

7. Add the split vanilla pod to the wine reduction (5) and whisk in 50 g (1¾ oz) of cold butter. Check the seasoning and strain through a fine sieve. Keep warm.

FINISHING THE DISH

8. Carve off the breast fillets of the duck and finish cooking the legs in a small sauté pan with a knob of butter. Put the fillets on two heated plates with two roasted pear halves each and pour over the red wine sauce (7). When the legs are cooked through, serve them with a salad of lamb's lettuce with a vinaigrette dressing.

* You could slice the fillets of duck breast before serving them. It could well look more elegant.
* Wild duck is always served with the breast meat cooked to a rare state and the legs well cooked.
* Figs can be used instead of pears.

Editor's note Although it is essential to serve wild duck rosy, 12 minutes cooking time might be too little for the tastes of some people, in which case allow an extra 5 minutes in the oven for a less rare result.

Perdrix rôtis à la sauge
Roast Partridge with Sage

Preparation time: 1½ hours
Oven temperature: 450°F/230°C/Gas 8

For two
people

2 young partridges (grey-legged if possible)
8 fresh sage leaves
4 slices of fresh belly of pork
1 medium-sized celeriac
2 tablespoons flour
150 g (5 oz) butter
2 eggs, beaten
100 g (3½ oz) fine fresh breadcrumbs
2 shallots, chopped
salt, freshly ground pepper

PRELIMINARY PREPARATIONS
1. The partridges should have been cleaned and plucked by the game-dealer. If not, you will have to do it yourself. Loosen the skin of the breast and push the sage leaves under the skin, four to each bird. Season the partridges inside and out with salt and pepper. Secure the pork fat over the breasts with fine string and set the birds aside. Preheat the oven.

2. Peel the celeriac and cut into sticks ¼" thick. Poach these "chips" in boiling salted water until they are still slightly crisp, drain and set aside.

ROASTING THE PARTRIDGE
3. Roast the partridge in the hot oven for 17 minutes, coating with 50 g (1¾ oz) butter at the beginning and basting with the cooking juices frequently as the birds cook.

4. Meanwhile, roll the celeriac chips in flour, then in beaten egg and finally in the breadcrumbs. Put aside ready for frying.

MAKING THE SAUCE
5. When the partridge are roasted, remove the string and the bards of pork. Cut each bird in half, remove the breasts and thighs and crush the bones in a pestle and mortar or with a cleaver. Pour off excess fat from the roasting pan and put in the bones with the chopped shallots and a knob of butter. When the bones are lightly browned, add 250 ml (scant half pint) water

and reduce until you have a rich sauce. Taste for seasoning, strain and keep very hot.

FRYING THE CELERIAC CHIPS AND SERVING THE PARTRIDGE
6. Heat a good lump of butter in a frying pan and fry the celeriac chips (4). Drain them on kitchen paper and sprinkle wih salt before arranging on a serving dish. Serve the breasts and thighs of the partridges coated with their hot sauce.

* The bards of belly of pork can be used, diced in a salad of frizzy endive.
* If you are lucky enough to obtain genuine wild birds (as opposed to farmed partridges) this is a marvellous recipe. But great care must be taken to time the cooking of the birds correctly. The flesh should still be rosy.

Poule faisane en tourte, aux salsifis et truffes
Hen Pheasant Cooked in a Crust, with Salsify and Truffles

Preparation time: 2½ hours
Oven temperature: 350°F/180°C/Gas 4

For four people
1 young hen pheasant, dressed
120 g (4½ oz) butter
100 g (3½ oz) belly of pork, diced
4 whole shallots, peeled
1 kg (2¼ lbs) salsify
80 g (3½ oz) fresh or preserved truffles
lemon juice
1 tablespoon flour
1 carrot, chopped
2 shallots, chopped
500 ml (scant pint) dry white wine
250 ml (scant half pint) port
2 tablespoons truffle juice
300 g (10½ oz) puff pastry
1 egg
salt, freshly ground pepper

"Un plat qui rappelle le 'chicken-pie'."

1. Cut the pheasant into four pieces and season with salt and pepper. Brown them in a large sauté pan with half the butter, the diced belly of pork and four whole shallots. When they have browned on the outside drain everything and set on one side. Do not wash the pan.

2. Wash the salsify in warm water and peel them with a potato-peeler. Blanch them in salted water with a few drops of lemon juice to which you have added 1 tablespoon of flour. Bring to the boil and cook for a full five minutes. Drain.

3. Remove the bones from the pieces of pheasant. Chop up the carcasses and set meat and bones aside separately.

FILLING THE PIE

4. Cut the salsify into pieces 2″ long and slice the truffles finely. Butter an oval earthenware terrine or pie dish and arrange the salsify, the pieces of pheasant and the slices of truffle in it. Season with salt and pepper.

MAKING THE SAUCE

5. Heat the pan in which the pheasant was cooked (1) and add the remaining butter, the crushed pheasant carcasses, the chopped shallots and carrot. Moisten with the white wine and reduce to half its volume. Then add the port and the truffle juice and reduce by half again. Strain through a fine sieve, pressing the shallots and carcasses with a spoon to extract all their juices. Pour over the pheasant and salsify and allow to cool.

COVERING AND COOKING THE PIE

6. Preheat the oven. Roll out the pastry to make a lid for the earthenware dish, leaving a wide margin. Allow to rest in the refrigerator for 15 minutes. Meanwhile, beat the egg with a tablespoon of water and brush the edges of the dish. Put on the pastry cover and seal by pressing down the edges firmly. Make a little hole ¾″ across in the middle of the pastry lid, brush with beaten egg and bake for 1½ hours. Serve straight from the oven.

* The pastry crust need not be eaten – it is simply a "shell" to keep in the delicious aromas.

Cailles "d'une bouchée"
Roast Quails

Preparation time: 1½ hours
Oven temperature: 475°F/240°C/Gas 9

For two
people

4 quails
100 g (4 oz) spinach
75 g (3 oz) butter
2 firm white button mushrooms, chopped
2 slices belly of pork, finely diced
1 shallot, chopped
2 chicken livers
1 tablespoon olive oil
1 clove garlic, 4 juniper berries
4 slices of bread, crusts removed

1. Pluck, singe and gut the quails, keeping aside the livers and hearts. Using your little finger, remove the bones of the birds from the inside, taking care not to break the skin. Keep the bones on one side and season the birds inside and out with salt and pepper.

2. Cook the spinach in boiling salted water, refresh and drain it. Squeeze the spinach hard and chop it finely with a knife.

3. Melt the butter in a sauté pan and add the chopped mushrooms, diced belly of pork and chopped shallot. Brown over a low heat, then add the chopped chicken livers and the hearts and livers of the quails. Stir, season with salt and pepper and allow to cool. Preheat the oven to its highest setting.

4. When the mixture is cold, add the spinach and chopped garlic and stuff each bird. Secure them with fine string so that the openings are sealed and cook them in a very hot oven, with their bones arranged round them, for 5-6 minutes. Baste with a mixture of olive oil and butter.

5. Remove the birds to a heated serving dish and keep hot. Crush the juniper berries and throw them into the roasting juices. Toast the 4 slices of bread, and sprinkle them generously with the juniper-scented pan juices. Serve beside the birds with a salad of curly endive with chopped herbs.

PASTA AND VEGETABLES

Pâtes fraîches et raviolis
Fresh Pasta and Ravioli

The Côte d'Azur is the prime region of France for the making and eating of pasta, and each chef tries to outdo his colleagues in finding new and ingenious ways of serving pasta. Nice was an Italian city until 1850 and the taste for pasta has remained, the recipes being passed from family to family.

Here are two recipes, one for fettuccine, lasagne and other kinds of fresh pasta and the other for making stuffed pastas such as ravioli. They were previously made mainly by housewives, whose fingers had acquired dexterity from years of practice, but now we have pasta-making machines and almost anyone can make good home-made pasta. For best results we use Italian machines for kneading, mixing and forcing the dough through a variety of rollers and perforated plates to make shells, noodles, macaroni, lasagne . . .

Basic Pasta Recipes

1. *For Fettuccine, Pasta Shells, Macaroni and Lasagne etc.*

250 g (8¾ oz) sifted flour
1 egg yolk
1 tablespoon olive oil
a pinch of salt
3 tablespoons water
1 strip of lemon peel

2. *For Ravioli, Cannelloni and Other Stuffed Pastas*

250 g (8¾ oz) sifted flour
2 small eggs (125 g/4 oz in all)
1 tablespoon softened lard
scant teaspoon white wine vinegar
salt, pepper

METHOD

The method is the same for both these recipes. Make a "well" in the flour and mix in the egg(s), fat or oil, salt and liquid. Knead thoroughly and when the dough is smooth, form into a ball and put in a cool place for 1-2 hours before using.

* There are a number of gadgets such as a special tray for making ravioli and other special cutters for noodles and other pastas, which make things easier for the cook.

Ravioli de homard à la moutarde et le bouillon de crustacés
Lobster Ravioli with Mustard and Shellfish Sauce

Preparation time: 3 hours

For four people
500 g (18 oz) ravioli dough (Recipe 2, *page 189*)
1 lobster weighing 700 to 800 g (1½-1¾ lbs)
200 g (7 oz) butter
200 g (7 oz) mushrooms, cleaned and quartered
3 tablespoons double cream or crème fraîche
1 tablespoon Dijon mustard
2 shallots, peeled and finely chopped
1 carrot, scraped and finely chopped
3 tablespoons dry white wine
salt, freshly ground pepper

"Un mélange homard-moutarde 'provocant' mais tellement subtil qu'il ne nuit en rien au goût puissant du homard qui est rehaussé par le bouillon l'accompagnant."

MAKING THE LOBSTER STUFFING

1. Plunge the lobster alive into boiling water for 5 minutes. Remove and allow to cool. Remove the flesh from the tail and claws and keep the shell for the sauce.

2. Melt 50 g (1¾ oz) butter in a sauté pan and brown the lobster meat lightly. Add the mushrooms and stir. Season with salt and pepper.

3. Mix the cream with the mustard and a tablespoon of water. Pour over the lobster, cover and cook very gently for 20-25 minutes. Mince coarsely and allow to cool.

MAKING THE SHELLFISH SAUCE

4. Meanwhile, make the lobster broth. Crush the shells of the lobster with a rolling pin or bottle. Sweat the finely chopped shallot and carrot in 50 g (1¾ oz) butter and add the crushed lobster shells. Moisten with the wine and 500 ml (scant pint) water and season with salt and pepper. Bring to the boil and simmer, skimming, until the liquid has reduced by half. Strain into a saucepan and return to the boil. Whisk in 100 g (3½ oz) diced cold butter and set aside in a warm place.

MAKING AND SERVING THE RAVIOLI

5. Roll out the pasta dough into two very thin sheets and put regularly spaced teaspoonfuls of the lobster stuffing (3) on one sheet. Using a pastry brush dipped in cold water, paint round each little heap of stuffing and spread the second sheet of pasta dough on top of the first. Seal round each teaspoon of stuffing with your thumb and cut into squares with a rotary ravioli cutter. Cook for 4-5 minutes in boiling salted water. Drain and divide between four heated plates. Reheat the sauce if necessary and pour over the ravioli.

* A tablespoon of oil added to the cooking water helps prevent the ravioli sticking together.

Ravioli de tapioca aux foies de volaille
Ravioli stuffed with Chicken Livers and Tapioca

Preparation time: 3 hours

For four
people

4 large chicken livers
100 g (3½ oz) butter
2 shallots, peeled and finely chopped
50 g (1¾ oz) tapioca
1 chicken stock cube dissolved in 1 litre (1¾ pints) water
2 tablespoons finely chopped chervil
5 egg yolks
500 g (18 oz) pasta dough (Recipe 2, *page 189*)
3 tablespoons double cream or crème fraîche
juice of 1 lemon
salt, freshly ground pepper

For method, see page 193.

Duck Roasted with garlic (page 178)

Fresh Noodles with Beans and Mussels (page 200)

Spinach Saint-Honoré (page 202)
Artichoke and Potato Rissoles (page 208)
Savoury Apple Clafoutis (page 213)

Pancakes Nicole Seitz (page 230)
Apples with Cider Butter (page 220)

1. Rinse, drain and dry the chicken livers. Heat 50 g (1¾ oz) butter in a frying pan and when it begins to turn golden put in the chicken livers and the chopped shallots. Cook them briefly, remove and drain.

2. Poach the tapioca in the boiling chicken stock, and when it has turned transparent remove it with a slotted spoon, keeping the stock.

3. Purée the chicken livers and shallots by rubbing them through a fine sieve into a bowl and add the poached tapioca, chopped chervil, 2 of the egg yolks and 50 g (1¾ oz) melted butter. Season with salt and pepper, mix well and allow to cool.

4. Roll out the pasta dough into two very, very fine sheets and put regularly-spaced teaspoonfuls of the stuffing on one sheet. Using a pastry brush dipped in cold water, paint round each little heap of stuffing and place the second sheet of pasta over the first. Seal each ravioli with your thumb and cut with a rotary pasta cutter. Cook in boiling salted water for 4-5 minutes.

5. Meanwhile reduce the reserved stock (2) by half. Mix the remaining 3 egg yolks with the cream in a small pan and pour on the reduced stock. Mix and thicken over a very low heat, stirring all the time. Season with salt and pepper and add the juice of 1 lemon.

6. Drain the ravioli, divide them between four heated soup plates and pour the sauce over them.

* A simpler sauce can be made by substituting 100 g (3½ oz) butter for the egg yolks and cream.

"Garniture indispensable d'un bouillon de volaille ou en entreé."

Ravioli de cèpes et de pied de veau
Wild Mushroom Ravioli

Preparation time: 3 hours

For four people
1 calf's foot, boned by the butcher
200 g (7 oz) fresh or frozen cèpes
3 shallots and 2 carrots, peeled and finely chopped
200 g (7 oz) butter
500 g (18 oz) ravioli dough (Recipe 2, *page 189*)
1 tablespoon chopped chervil
salt, freshly ground pepper

"Une recette à faire en pleine période des cèpes (août-septembre) pour en apprécier pleinement la saveur."

1. Wash the boned calf's foot in cold running water and bring to the boil in water salted with a handful of coarse salt. When it boils, remove the calf's foot, refresh under cold running water, and drain. Cut into cubes as soon as it is cool enough. Clean and halve the cèpes.

2. Sweat the chopped vegetables in 100 g (3½ oz) butter in a sauté pan, and when they are soft add the cubed calf's foot and the halved cèpes. Season with salt and pepper, add 500 ml (scant pint) water, cover and simmer for 2 hours on a low heat. Stir from time to time and add a little more water if necessary.

3. Strain the contents of the pan, reserving the cooking liquid in a saucepan, which should be returned to the stove to reduce by half. Mince the meat, cèpes and vegetables through the fine blade of a mincer, chop briefly in a food processor or chop as finely as possible with a knife. Let the mixture cool while you roll out the pasta dough into two very fine sheets (the dough should be almost transparent).

4. Place regularly-spaced teaspoonfuls of the cooled stuffing on one of the sheets. Using a pastry-brush dipped in cold water, paint round each little heap of stuffing and place the second sheet of pasta over the first. Seal round each ravioli with your thumb and cut into square ravioli with a rotary pasta cutter. Poach in boiling salted water for 4-5 minutes.

5. When the strained cooking liquid (3) has reduced by half, whisk in 100 g (3½ oz) of cold diced butter. Bring to the boil again, check the seasoning and skim.

6. Divide the cooked, strained ravioli between 4 heated soup plates and cover with the sauce. Sprinkle with a little chopped chervil at the last moment.

Ravioli de coquilles saint-jacques aux poireaux
Ravioli stuffed with scallops and leeks

Preparation time: 3 hours

For four
people

500 g (18 oz) pasta dough (Recipe 2, *page 189*)
500 g (18 oz) white parts of leeks
1 kg (2¼ lbs) scallops in their shells
230 g (8 oz) butter
2 egg yolks
1 tablespoon double cream or crème fraîche
2 shallots, peeled and chopped
250 ml (scant half pint) dry white wine
1 tablespoon finely chopped chervil
juice of 1 lemon
cayenne pepper
2 teaspoons chopped chives
salt, freshly ground pepper

"Une excellente entrée ou un accompagnement idéal d'un plat de poisson en guise de garniture."

1. Cut the leeks lengthways and rinse under cold running water. Slice them finely and sweat in 100 g (3½ oz) butter in a large sauté pan.

2. Remove the scallops from their shells, trim them and rinse under cold running water. Chop them medium-fine with a knife or in a food-processor. Drain in a colander.

MAKING THE STUFFING
3. Mix the egg yolks, cream, chopped chervil and drained minced scallops in a bowl. Mix well, season with salt and pepper and add to the leeks in the sauté pan. Stir, and cook for 1 minute. Drain in a colander placed over a bowl, and allow to cool.

MAKING AND COOKING THE RAVIOLI
4. Roll out the pasta dough as finely as possible into two sheets. Place regularly-spaced teaspoonfuls of the cooled stuffing on one of the sheets. Using a pastry-brush dipped in cold water, paint round each little heap of stuffing and place the second sheet of dough over the first. Seal each ravioli around with your thumb and cut into squares with a rotary pasta-cutter. Poach in boiling salted water for 4-5 minutes.

FINISHING AND SERVING THE PASTA
5. Meanwhile, finish the sauce. Soften the chopped shallots in 30 g (1 oz) butter in a small pan. Add the wine and reduce over a brisk heat until the liquid has almost evaporated. Add the reserved cooking juices (3), bring to the boil and whisk in 100 g (3½ oz) cold diced butter. When the sauce has amalgamated, adjust the seasoning with lemon juice, cayenne pepper and salt. Drain the ravioli and divide them between four heated soup plates. Pour the sauce over the pasta and sprinkle with chopped chives.

Cannelloni à la brousse et au basilic
Cannelloni with Brousse and Basil

Preparation time: 1 hour
Oven temperature: 375°F/190°C/Gas 5

*For four
people*

500 g (18 oz) ravioli dough (Recipe 2, *page 189*)
600 g (1 lb 5 oz) brousse *or* other low fat fresh cow's milk cheese such
   as ricotta
1 clove of garlic, peeled and chopped
2 tablespoons chopped fresh basil (14 leaves)
50 g (1¾ oz) pine-nuts
a dash of marc de Provence *or* other marc
100 g (3½ oz) thinly sliced Comté (*or* Gruyère *or* Emmenthal) cheese
150g (3½ oz) softened butter
250 ml (scant ½ pint) whipping cream
juice of ½ lemon
salt, freshly ground pepper

1. Preheat the oven. Roll out the pasta dough as finely as possible and cut into rectangles 4″ long by 3″. Poach the rectangles for approximately 3 minutes in boiling salted water, refresh under cold water and spread out to drain on a cloth.

2. Mix the brousse, which should be well drained, with the chopped garlic, half the basil and the pine-nuts. Season with salt and pepper and add a dash of marc. Spread a tablespoonful of this stuffing in a long cork shape on each rectangle of pasta and roll them up.

3. Butter an earthenware gratin dish and put in the cannelloni in a single layer. Sprinkle with 50 g (2 oz) melted butter and place a paper-thin slice of cheese over each cannelloni. Bake in the oven for 30 minutes.

4. Meanwhile, make a little accompanying sauce. Mix the remaining basil with 100 g (3½ oz) softened butter. Bring the cream to the boil in a pan and, off the heat, whisk in the basil butter vigorously. Add the lemon juice, season with salt and pepper and keep warm in a sauceboat.

5. Serve the cannelloni in the dish they have cooked in, and serve the sauce separately.

* Brousse is a mild, fresh, white cheese, usually made with sheep or goat's milk. Originally Provençal it is widely appreciated in the Mediterranean in autumn, winter and spring. There is also a Corsican version called Broccio Corse Frais. It is, rather like ricotta, delicious eaten with fruit or in savoury dishes.

L'embeurrée de fettuccine aux fevettes et aux moules
Noodles with Baby Broad Beans and Mussels

Preparation time: 1 hour

For four
people

1 kg (2¼ lbs) mussels in their shells
1 kg (2¼ lbs) baby broad beans
500 g (18 oz) pasta dough (Recipe 1, *page 189*)
100 g (3½ oz) brousse *or* ricotta (*see note page 199*)
1 teaspoon chopped basil (10 leaves)
salt, freshly ground pepper

PRELIMINARY PREPARATIONS
1. Scrape and wash the mussels and open them by placing them over a moderate heat in a large covered pan with a very little water and a grinding of black pepper (no salt). When they have opened, and cooked for 2-3 minutes, remove them, discarding any which have failed to open and keeping the cooking liquid on one side. Shell the mussels.

2. Remove the bean pods and peel off the fine skin which envelops each bean.

ROLLING OUT AND COOKING THE PASTA
3. Roll out the pasta dough very finely and cut into strips ¼″ wide and 11-12″ long. Poach them in boiling salted water for 2 minutes. Refresh them under cold water and drain.

FINISHING AND SERVING THE PASTA
4. Mash the cheese with a fork. Bring the reserved juices from the mussels to the boil and add the mashed cheese, the mussels, the beans and the pasta. Stir with a fork and when the mixture is hot, pile it into a serving bowl, sprinkle with chopped basil and serve immediately.

* A speck of crushed garlic added at Step 1 will give extra flavour.

"Des pâtes comme on les aime dans le Midi."

Gratin de "Jo"
Jo's Gratin

Preparation time: 2 hours
Oven temperature: 400°F/200°C/Gas 6

For four people

1 kg (2¼ lbs) waxy potatoes
1 litre (1¾ pints) semi-skimmed milk
250 g (9 oz) butter
1 clove of garlic, peeled
1 litre (1¾ pints) whipping cream
salt, freshly ground pepper

PREPARING THE POTATOES

1. Peel the potatoes with a potato-peeler. Wash them and cut in two lengthwise, then into very fine slices, ⅛" thick.

2. Butter a large sauté pan and pour in the milk. Season with salt and pepper. Lay the potato slices in the milk and dot with butter. Simmer for approximately 20 minutes. Preheat the oven.

3. Rub a round or oval earthenware gratin dish with garlic, and butter the bottom and sides lavishly.

FINISHING AND SERVING THE GRATIN

4. When the potatoes are tender, but still slightly crisp, remove them from the sauté pan with a slotted spoon and arrange them in layers in the gratin dish. Cover with the cream, dot with butter, season with pepper and bake in the oven for approximately 1 hour. The potatoes will absorb the cream and their starch will bind the liquid. The gratin will be golden and glazed on the top, ready to serve at once.

* It is vital that the potatoes are sliced really finely – with a knife or a mandoline – and that they are neither rinsed nor dried.

" 'Jo' Rostang, célèbre restaurateur, en sa Bonne Auberge à Antibes, réalise, entre autres, le plus merveilleux des gratins dauphinois."

Saint-honoré aux épinards
Spinach Saint-Honoré

Preparation time: 1½ hours
Oven temperature: 450°F/230°C/Gas 8

For six
people
2 kg (4 lb 6 oz) fresh leaf spinach
20 small pickling onions
150 g (5¼ oz) butter
1 tablespoon sugar
200 g (7 oz) mushrooms
350 ml (⅔ pint) whipping cream
2 eggs
50 g (1¾ oz) split almonds
salt, freshly ground pepper

"En tout point similaire au Saint-Honoré de pâtisserie pour le dressage. Seuls les
éléments constituant la recette changent."

PREPARING THE SPINACH PURÉE
1. Remove the stalks from the spinach, wash it thoroughly and plunge into a pan of heavily salted boiling water. Let it boil uncovered for 2 minutes, then drain and refresh it. Squeeze with your hands to remove as much moisture as possible then liquidise to a smooth purée. Set aside.

COOKING THE ONIONS
2. Preheat the oven. Peel the onions and cook with 50 g (1¾ oz) butter, a tablespoon of sugar and enough water to cover. Simmer, covered, until the liquid has reduced to a syrup, coating the onions.

MAKING THE MUSHROOM "CAKE"
3. Meanwhile, trim the mushrooms and chop them finely. Fry them with 50 g (1¾ oz) butter until they give up their juices. Drain them and, while they are still hot, purée them. Pour the purée into a bowl and add all but 3 tablespoons of the cream, the beaten eggs, salt and pepper. Mix well and pour into a buttered sponge tin. Set the tin in a roasting pan of hot water and bake in the oven for 15-20 minutes.

FINISHING AND SERVING THE SAINT-HONORÉ
4. When the mushroom cake is nearly cooked, toast the almonds until they are pale golden and add them to the glazed onions (2), stirring them in carefully. Turn out the cooked mushroom cake onto a large round plate and arrange the onions round the edge in a coronet. Keep hot while you reheat the spinach purée (1) and mix in 50 g (1¾ oz) of diced cold butter and the remaining cream. Season with salt and pepper and pipe rapidly in a rosette pattern over the top of the mushroom cake, using a pastry bag.

5. Reheat in a hot oven for a few seconds if necessary and serve with a baked fish or a fish with sauce, or on its own with a hollandaise.

* The little glazed onions should be golden brown.
* The mushroom cake should be approximately 1" thick.

Ratatouille de J.M.
Ratatouille "J.M."

Preparation time: 1½ hours

For from four to six people

2 glossy elongated aubergines
2 long courgettes
5 large very ripe tomatoes
1 onion
2 red and 2 green peppers
a deep frying pan of vegetable oil for skinning the peppers
1 small Florence fennel bulb
5 cloves of garlic
1 leek
a bouquet garni (1 sprig of celery, bayleaf, 1 sprig of thyme, 5 basil
    leaves and a sage leaf tied with thread)
500 ml (scant pint) olive oil
salt, freshly ground pepper

"J.M. – J. comme Jacques, M. comme Maximin ou Médecin . . . Devinez!"

1. Wipe the courgettes and aubergines with a cloth and cut them into cubes the size of sugar lumps.

2. Plunge the peppers into boiling vegetable oil for 2 minutes and peel them when they have cooled down. Remove the pips and white pith and cut them into even pieces the size of the courgettes.

3. Plunge the tomatoes into boiling water for 10 seconds, refresh them under cold running water and peel them. Remove the seeds and cut into dice.

4. Chop the onion, fennel and leek as finely as you can. Peel the cloves of garlic and crush them by flattening them with your hand. Assemble the bouquet garni.

5. Cook the aubergine, courgette and peppers separately in very hot olive oil until they are lightly browned. Drain and set aside.

6. Heat 250 ml (scant ½ pint) olive oil in a large shallow sauté pan or casserole, and add the chopped onion, fennel and leek with the bouquet garni. Allow them to soften over a moderate heat, then add the chopped tomatoes and garlic. Season with salt and pepper, cover with foil and a lid and simmer until the tomatoes have melted and thickened. Then add the aubergines, courgettes and peppers and simmer, still covered, over a low heat for 45 minutes.

* 1 teaspoon of tomato concentrate mixed with a little water can be added to improve the colour.
* This ratatouille can be eaten hot with lamb, or other roast meat or poultry, and is equally good cold.

Cake aux légumes
Vegetable Cake

Preparation time: 1½ hours
Oven temperature: 1. 450°F/230°C/Gas 8, 2. 350°F/180°C/Gas 4

For from six 70 g (2½ oz) carrots
to eight 70 g (2½ oz) courgettes
people 70 g (2½ oz) mushrooms
200 g (7 oz) softened butter
6 eggs
250 g (9 oz) flour
1 teaspoon baking powder
celery salt
grated zest of 1 orange and 1 lemon
salt, freshly ground pepper

PREPARING THE VEGETABLES

1. Peel the carrots and courgettes, cut them into medium-size dice and cook them separately in boiling salted water, refresh and drain. Clean and trim the mushrooms, dice them and cook for 30 seconds in hot butter. Drain.

2. Dry the vegetables in a medium oven for about 15 minutes and meanwhile place the 6 eggs in a bowl of tepid water to bring them up to room temperature.

MAKING THE CAKE

3. Put the softened butter in a bowl and mix in the eggs one by one, stirring constantly so that you have a smooth mixture.

4. Preheat the oven. Roll the dried vegetables in the flour, then sieve the flour into a bowl, keeping the vegetables on one side. Add the baking powder to the flour and season with celery salt and salt and pepper. Sieve the flour onto the butter and eggs (3) stirring with a wooden spoon and finally add the floured vegetables and the grated zests of a lemon and an orange.

BAKING AND SERVING THE CAKE

5. Butter a cake tin, pour in the mixture and bake for 10 minutes in the hot oven. Then lower the oven setting and bake for a further 45 minutes. Turn out the cake and let it cool before slicing.

* The cake can be stored in the refrigerator, wrapped in plastic wrap.
* This cake is a happy alternative to toast and brioche when a pâté or terrine is being served. It can also be used for the making of canapés.

Editor's note You can also add skinned red peppers cut into cubes to the other vegetables for colour.

Palets d'artichauts et de pommes de terre
Artichoke and Potato Rissoles

Preparation time: 1½ hours

For four people
4 artichokes, preferably the violet variety
2 large waxy potatoes in their skins
50 g (1¾ oz) flour
1 egg, beaten
100 g (3½ oz) white breadcrumbs
50 g (1¾ oz) butter
salt, freshly ground pepper

PREPARING THE VEGETABLES
1. Place the artichokes and potatoes in their skins in two saucepans of cold salted water and bring to the boil. Cook until just tender. Test the potatoes by piercing with the point of a knife and the artichokes by removing a leaf, which should come away easily.

2. Peel the potatoes and cut in paper-thin slices ⅛" thick. Remove the leaves and chokes of the artichokes and cut the hearts into slices of the same thickness as the potatoes.

MAKING THE RISSOLES
3. Build the slices up into little rissoles ¾" thick, alternating potato and artichoke. Press the rissoles with the palm of your hand to firm them, then roll in flour, then seasoned beaten egg and finally in the breadcrumbs.

FRYING AND SERVING THE RISSOLES
4. Just before serving, heat the butter in a frying-pan and fry the rissoles on both sides for 2 minutes. Drain on kitchen paper and season with salt and pepper. Serve immediately with any kind of roast meat or poultry.

* Any number of different vegetables can be used in place of artichokes – for instance carrots, turnips, pumpkin or celeriac.

"Palets dorés et fondants, renfermant le parfum de l'artichaut violet et le moelleux de la pomme de terre cuite en 'robe'."

Gratin de navets aux pruneaux
Turnip Gratin with Prunes

Preparation time: 45 minutes
Oven temperature: 450°F/230°C/Gas 8

For four people

10 small turnips – about 1 kg (2¼ lbs)
100 g (3½ oz) butter
100 g (3½ oz) prunes
250 ml (scant ½ pint) double cream or crème fraîche
2 egg yolks
salt, freshly ground pepper

PREPARING THE GRATIN

1. Preheat the oven. Peel the turnips with a potato peeler and slice them finely. Soften in butter, season with salt and pepper and drain. Remove the stones from the prunes, cut them into small pieces and brown quickly in butter. Drain and mix with the cooked sliced turnips.

2. Transfer the mixture to a buttered shallow oval gratin dish 8″ long, pressing it down firmly with a fork. Bake for 5-6 minutes.

GLAZING AND COOKING THE GRATIN

3. Meanwhile, beat the cream with the egg yolks. Pour over the turnip and prune mixture and return the dish to the oven to brown. Serve immediately, from the cooking dish.

* The turnips should be well-drained and patted with paper towels so that they are as dry as possible.
* A perfect accompaniment for a roast leg of lamb or roast duck.

"Un gratin 'minute' dans lequel le parfum des navets reste intacte après une cuisson très courte."

Mousseline de brocoli huilée
Broccoli Purée with Hazel Nut Oil

Preparation time: 30 minutes

For four people

1 large head of green or purple broccoli (the ones that are the size of cauliflowers)
6-7 tablespoons olive oil
3 tablespoons hazel nut oil
salt, freshly ground pepper

1. Remove any green leaves from the broccoli. Separate the florets and cook until very tender in boiling salted water – for about 15-20 minutes.

2. Remove the florets with a slotted spoon and purée with the two kinds of oil. Season with salt and pepper and serve as soon as possible as an accompaniment to a grilled fish or a roast joint.

* The broccoli should be well cooked, and puréed whilst it is still hot.
* This is an excellent purée to accompany fish, but delicious too with game – medallions of venison for example.

Dragées de gousses d'ail
Garlic Croquettes

Preparation time: 1½ hours

For four people

20 cloves of garlic
6 hard-boiled egg yolks
50 g (1¾ oz) softened butter
1 leaf of fresh basil, finely chopped
2 tablespoons flour
2 eggs, beaten
1 tablespoon oil
100 g (3½ oz) bread crumbs
oil for frying
salt, freshly ground pepper

1. Blanch the peeled cloves of garlic in three changes of boiling water. (They should be well cooked.) Refresh them in cold water and purée. Pour the purée into a bowl and add the softened butter and the basil. Sieve the egg yolks on to the mixture and beat with a wooden spoon until quite smooth. Form the mixture into little balls the size of a marble and put them to harden in the freezer on a sheet of foil.

2. When the garlic balls are very firm, roll them first in the flour, then in a mixture of 2 eggs beaten with 1 tablespoon of oil, and one of water, seasoned with salt and pepper (this mixture is called "une anglaise"). Shake off any excess liquid and roll the balls in the breadcrumbs, shaping them with your fingers to look like cloves of garlic.

3. Just before serving, fry the "dragées" and hand them separately with the Rabbit with Girolles on page 158.

* With a little practice, you can shape the dragées in Step 1 quite quickly by using a forcing bag to pipe garlic shapes on to a sheet of foil.

"Des petites dragées moelleuses qui n'ont pas, comme ou pourvait le penser, un dominance d'ail!"

"Pan bagnat" au pommes rapées
"Pan Bagnat" of Apples

Preparation time: 15 minutes

For four people
4 round flat rolls
50 g (1¾ oz) duck fat
4 lettuce leaves
2 eating apples, peeled, cored and grated
salt, freshly ground pepper

Cut the rolls in half and toast the cut sides lightly. While they are still hot, spread each piece with a thin layer of duck fat. Season with salt and pepper. Spread a lettuce leaf out on each lower half and sprinkle with grated apple. Salt lightly and replace the top halves of the loaves to make a sandwich. Serve immediately, while they are still warm.

* The loaves should be well risen, and preferably cooked in a wood oven.
* A trickle of walnut or hazel nut oil can be used instead of duck fat.
* This famous Niçois sandwich has been debased by unscrupulous traders, but is delicious when properly made in the traditional manner. This is a variation which I serve with a slice of foie gras or a terrine.

Editor's note Pan Bagnat rolls are round, flat, slightly uneven white rolls, usually at least 6" and sometimes up to 12" across. A good home-made Pan Bagnat makes an excellent lunch.

Clafoutis de reinettes salé
Savoury Apple Clafoutis

Preparation time: 35 minutes
Oven temperature: 400°F/200°C/Gas 6

For four people

2 reinette apples (russets)
50 g (1¾ oz) butter
2 eggs
4 tablespoons double cream or crème fraîche
salt, freshly ground pepper

1. Preheat the oven. Peel, core and slice the apples. Melt the butter in a frying pan and sauté the apples briefly, without letting them brown too much. When they are soft, remove them and allow to cool.

2. Meanwhile, mix the eggs and the cream in a bowl and season with salt and pepper. Stir in the cooled apples. Butter four 4″ round tartlet tins and divide the mixture between them. Bake in the oven for 15 minutes.

3. Turn out the clafoutis as soon as they are cooked and serve just as they are. An ideal accompaniment for a terrine of fresh foie gras.

* Golden Delicious apples can also be used.
* Salted, they make a delicious garnish for a savoury dish, but they can also be served, sprinkled with sugar, as a pudding.

DESSERTS

Mousse aux fraises des bois
Wild Strawberry Mousse

Preparation time: 30 minutes plus chilling time

For six people
250 g (scant half pint) whipping cream (crème fleurette)
3 leaves of gelatine
3 egg whites
150 g (5¼ oz) sugar
250 g (9 oz) wild strawberries, puréed

1. Whip the cream and chill it.

2. Soften the gelatine in a little cold water for ten minutes.

3. Cook the sugar with a little water until it reaches 250°F/121°C, hard ball stage. Whip the egg whites to a snow and pour on the syrup whisking it in as you pour. Squeeze the water out of the gelatine and add it to the still hot "Italian" meringue, stirring it in thoroughly.

4. Mix half the fruit purée with the chilled whipped cream and the other half with the meringue. Then fold everything together and pour into individual ramekins or soufflé dishes.

5. Place the ramekins in the refrigerator to stiffen the mixture.

* You can use any red soft fruit for this recipe.
* For most mousses the use of "Italian" meringue makes for a lighter result and prevents them from sticking.
* Wild strawberries, when they are perfectly ripe, seem to me to be the ideal fruit for mousses of this kind. Their inimitable fragrance and penetrating flavours stand up well to the addition of whipped cream without losing any of their strength.

For a note on gelatine, see Introduction.

Terrine d'oranges sanguines au champagne
Terrine of Blood Oranges with Champagne

Preparation time: 45 minutes plus chilling time

For ten people

15 blood oranges
9 leaves of gelatine
500 ml (scant pint) blood orange juice
500 ml (scant pint) champagne

1. Peel the oranges, removing the skin and all the white pith. Skin the segments and put them to dry a little spread out on a cloth.

2. Soften the gelatine for ten minutes in a little cold water. Squeeze out the water and melt it in a little orange juice over a low flame. When the gelatine is thoroughly melted mix in the rest of the orange juice, chilled, and the champagne. Allow the mixture to cool, without setting, stirring it over a bowl of ice if you are short of time.

3. Cover the bottom of a rectangular terrine with orange segments. Pour over enough of the orange juice and champagne to cover, and chill. Repeat this operation until the terrine is full. Chill until the jelly has set firmly, and serve cut in slices.

* If you have time, I advise you to prepare the orange segments the night before. The longer they have to dry, the better they will stick to the jelly, giving a firm terrine which will not fall apart when cut.

Gratin de fraises des bois "Yves Thuries"
Strawberry and Lemon Gratins "Yves Thuries"

Preparation time: 1 hour

For ten people

200 ml (17 fl oz) fresh lemon juice
125 g (4½ oz) double cream
6 egg yolks
250 g (8¾ oz) sugar
30 g (1 oz) flour
3 leaves of gelatine
6 egg whites
250 g (8¾ oz) wild strawberries

"Lors d'une croisière gastronomique, mon ami Yves Thuries nous époustoufla par son talent avec, entre autres, ce dessert. Il me communiqua la recette. Un juste hommage lui est rendu ici."

MAKING THE LEMON CREAM

1. Bring the lemon juice and cream to the boil. Beat the egg yolks with 50 g (1¾ oz) of the sugar and the flour. Pour the boiling cream onto the egg yolks. Mix and bring back almost to the boil.

2. Soften the gelatine for 10 minutes in cold water. Squeeze out excess moisture and stir into the hot lemon cream.

3. Cook the rest of the sugar with a little water until it reaches 244°F/117°C firm ball, and meanwhile whisk the egg whites to a snow. Pour on the sugar syrup, whisking all the time with an electric beater and beat until it is well mixed in and the mixture is cold. Fold in the lemon cream carefully.

FINISHING AND SERVING THE GRATINS

4. Set out 10 open circular moulds 4-4½″ in diameter on a sheet of baking paper. Fill each circle with a little lemon mousse, strew with wild strawberries and cover over with more mousse. Chill.

5. Just before you need them, remove the mould from each mousse carefully with a wet knife. Sprinkle with caster sugar and brown for a few seconds in a very hot oven or with a salamander.

* This dessert can be served with an orange butter sauce made by reducing a little orange juice and Grand Marnier and whisking in cubes of butter as if you were making a beurre blanc.
* A few wild strawberries make an attractive accompaniment.

Praline Negresco
Chocolate Floating Islands

Preparation time: 30 minutes plus chilling time

For four people
4 egg whites
200 g (7 oz) sugar
200 g (7 oz) dark cooking chocolate
50 g (1¾ oz) toasted chopped almonds
500 ml (scant pint) milk
6 egg yolks
80 g (2¾ oz) sugar
100 g (3½ oz) praline, crushed

MAKING THE MERINGUE ISLANDS
1. Mix the egg whites and the sugar together and heat gently, until they reach a temperature of 104°F/40°C. Beat the mixture until it has completely cooled. When the whites are stiff and airy, form into 4 rounds in a buttered ladle and drop gently into hot, but not boiling water (180°F/85°C) to poach for 20 minutes.

2. When the egg whites are cooked, let them cool on a cloth or paper towel and then put them on a dish. Melt the chocolate in a bain marie or double boiler and add the toasted almonds. Coat each "island" of egg white with the chocolate, and chill.

MAKING THE PRALINE SAUCE
3. Bring the milk to the boil while you beat the egg yolks with the sugar. Pour the milk on to the yolks, stir and return to the saucepan. Cook over a gentle heat without boiling, until the mixture coats the back of a spoon – about 3 minutes at 180°F/85°C – then whisk in the crushed praline powder. Cool over cracked ice or in the refrigerator.

4. Ladle some praline sauce into four bowls and float a chocolate-covered island in each.

Oeufs à la neige, sauce milkshake
Oeufs à la Neige with Milkshake Sauce

Preparation time: 1 hour
Oven temperature: 350°F/180°C/Gas 4

For six
people

8 egg whites
300 g (10½ oz) sugar
250 ml (scant half pint) homemade or good-quality bought raspberry
　　sorbet
200 ml (⅓ pint) milk
200 ml (⅓ pint) double cream
200 g (7 oz) raspberries

1. Preheat the oven. Whip the egg whites to a snow, add 200 g (7 oz) of the sugar and beat for several minutes more.

2. Butter a bowl and pour in the egg whites. Cook in a bain-marie or roasting pan filled with water for 30 minutes. Remove from the oven, turn out on a serving platter and allow to cool.

3. Blend the sorbet, the milk and the cream to make the "milkshake" sauce. Crush the raspberries with the remaining sugar and pass through a sieve to remove the seeds.

4. Pour the fruit purée over the egg whites and serve with the milkshake sauce.

* A pinch of salt added to the egg whites before whisking will prevent them from becoming grainy.
* You can equally well cook the egg whites in a large buttered ladle, plunged into simmering water.
* A different way of making "oeufs à la neige", fresh-tasting and very pleasant in summer. Fresh fruits such as mulberries, blackberries, wild strawberries and redcurrants can be served alongside.

Gratin de golden frangipane, beurre de cidre
Apples with Cider Butter

Preparation time: 30 minutes

For six people

For the Apples
4 Golden Delicious apples, peeled and sliced
500 g (18 oz) sugar
1 vanilla pod
juice of 1 lemon

For the Frangipane
100g (3½ oz) softened butter
500 g (18 oz) sugar
100 g (3½ oz) ground almonds
2 eggs

For the Cider Butter
2 Golden Delicious apples
200 g (7 oz) butter
250 ml (scant half pint) cider

"Un dessert automnal qui parachèvera un dîner de chasse."

1. Make a syrup from the sugar, vanilla pod and lemon juice with 1 litre (1¾ pints) water and use it to poach four peeled and finely sliced apples. Arrange the poached slices, overlapping in rosettes, on six small dessert plates and allow to cool. Preheat the grill.

2. Beat the butter and the sugar together to a cream, then add the almonds and the eggs and mix thoroughly. Pour a thin layer of this cream over the apple slices, and just before you serve the dish, place each plate under the grill and brown the top slightly.

3. Sweat the remaining peeled, cored and quartered apples in a little butter. Add the cider and cook gently until tender and reduced. Sieve the apple sauce thus obtained and purée with 200 g (7 oz) butter to make a delicate cider butter. Serve hot.

* The gratin must be glazed at the last moment, and the cider butter sauce served separately in a sauceboat.
* If you have no Golden Delicious apples, Russets can be substituted, provided you take care to poach them so that they remain slightly crisp.

Charlotte aux Kumquats
Kumquat Charlotte

Preparation time: 1¼ hours
Oven temperature: 400°F/200°C/Gas 6

For eight people

For the Sponge Base
4 eggs
160 g (5½ oz) caster sugar
160 g (5½ oz) flour

For the Kumquat Mousse
250 ml (scant ½ pint) whipping cream
4 leaves gelatine
3 egg whites
150 g (5¼ oz) sugar
250 g (9 oz) kumquat purée, pips removed

MAKING THE SPONGE

1. Preheat the oven. Separate the egg yolks and beat the whites to a soft snow. Fold in the sugar and beat a little more until the whites are firm. Fold in the yolks and then sift in the flour, folding it into the mixture with a spatula.

2. Butter a piece of silicone baking paper and pipe the mixture in a rectangle of little sausage shapes arranged in diagonal rows just touching each other. Bake for 5 minutes.

MAKING THE KUMQUAT MOUSSE

3. Whip the cream and put it to chill in the refrigerator. Soak the gelatine in cold water. Put the sugar and a little water in a small pan and heat to 245°F/121°C, hard ball stage. Beat the three whites to a snow and then pour the syrup over them in a thin stream, whisking it in as you do so.

4. Immediately, squeeze out the gelatine and fold it into the hot meringue mixture. Beat until the meringue is cold, transfer the mixture to a bowl and then fold in the kumquat purée and the whipped cream.

ASSEMBLING THE CHARLOTTE

5. Line a charlotte mould with the biscuit, using upright bands of biscuit for the sides, trimming them to the height of the mould, and cutting out a circle of biscuit for the bottom.

6. Fill the mould with the Kumquat Mousse (4), chill and turn out when you are ready to serve the charlotte.

* This charlotte should be eaten chilled and can be served with a bowl of kumquat purée sweetened with a syrup made with sugar and a little water.
* The kumquat is a neglected fruit, with a remarkable tart taste; equally good eaten as it is with its skin on, or rolled in fine sugar.

Gâteau aux noix
Walnut Cake

Preparation time: 1 hour plus chilling time
Oven temperature: 400°F/200°C/Gas 6

For eight people

For the Sponge Base
4 eggs
120 g (4¼ oz) sugar)
120 g (4¼ oz) flour, sifted
100 g (3½ oz) chopped walnuts
1 tablespoon coffee extract *or* very strong instant coffee (3 teaspoons
    instant coffee to 1 tablespoon water)

For the Bavarois
750 ml (1¼ pints) crème fleurette (whipping cream)
500 ml (17 fl oz) milk
8 egg yolks
350 g (12½ oz) sugar
1 tablespoon coffee extract *or* very strong instant coffee (as above)
6 leaves of gelatine
100 g (3½ oz) chopped walnuts

For the Syrup
200 g (7 oz) sugar
6½ tablespoons rum
biscuit crumbs

MAKING THE SPONGE BASE

1. Preheat the oven. Beat the eggs with the sugar, using an electric beater, until pale, heat in the top of a double boiler, beating all the time, until the temperature has reached 100°F/40°C. Remove from the heat and beat the mixture briskly to a thick foam as it cools. Sift the flour, add it to the nuts and mix well.

2. Add the tablespoon of coffee extract a little at a time to the egg mixture beating as you do so. Fold in the flour and nuts carefully without losing the light frothiness of the mixture.

3. Butter a baking tray and flour it lightly or cover it with baking paper. Spread out a layer of sponge ¾" thick, smoothing it with a spatula, cook for 8-10 minutes with the oven door just ajar.

4. Make a syrup by dissolving the sugar in the rum with 3-4 tablespoons water.

MAKING THE BAVAROIS

5. Whip the cream and chill. Bring the milk to the boil.

6. Whisk the egg yolks, the sugar and the coffee. Dilute with the milk. Pour into a saucepan and cook without boiling at a temperature of 180°F/85°C for 3 minutes, or until it coats the back of a spoon.

7. Soak the gelatine in cold water (about 10 minutes) until it is soft. Squeeze the gelatine dry and add to the hot Bavarois, mix well and then cool stirring, over a bowl of ice until the Bavarois thickens.

8. Fold in the chilled whipped cream and the nuts.

ASSEMBLING THE CAKE

9. Cut a circle from the sponge (3) to fit the bottom of a spring-clip cake tin. Make holes in the cake with a skewer and soak it with the syrup a few teaspoons at a time. Then top with the Bavarois cream (8). Remove the mould before serving.

* This dessert should be eaten very cold. It can be served with a coffee sauce made with a custard flavoured with coffee beans toasted in the oven and crushed.

Editor's note This can be made with half the quantity of cream for a less rich result.

Cheese Cake
Cheese Cake

Preparation time: 1½ hours
Oven temperature: 400°F/200°C/Gas 6

For eight people

The Sponge Base
4 eggs
120 g (4¼ oz) flour, sifted
120 g (4¼ oz) sugar

The Cheese Filling
800 g (1 lb 12 oz) whipping cream
600 g (1 lb 5 oz) fromage blanc
250 g (9 oz) sugar
5 egg yolks
8 leaves gelatine
200 g (7 oz) raspberry jelly *or* sieved raspberry jam

Editor's note The oven door can be kept slightly open with the handle of a spoon. This prevents the build up of moisture which would spoil the sponge base.

"La réhabilitation du goût américain, très allégé."

MAKING THE GENOISE (SPONGE) BASE

1. Mix together the four eggs and the sugar in a bowl, and warm them gently in the top of a double boiler, beating all the time, until the temperature reaches 100°F/40°C. Remove and beat the mixture continuously until it is cold. Fold in the sifted flour. Preheat the oven.

2. Spread out the base ¾" thick on a sheet of buttered greaseproof or baking paper on a baking sheet. Cook for 5 minutes with the oven door very slightly ajar.

MAKING THE CHEESE FILLING

3. Beat the cream until it forms stiff peaks. Fold in the fromage blanc and half the sugar.

4. Beat the egg yolks with the other half of the sugar. Soften the gelatine in a little cold water, drain it, and melt in a small saucepan on a very low heat.

5. Incorporate the egg yolks and sugar mixture in the whipped cream and cheese mixture and quickly mix in the melted gelatine.

ASSEMBLING THE CHEESE CAKE

6. Cut out a circle, the diameter of a spring-clip cake mould, from the Genoise base and spread this sponge base with raspberry jelly or sieved raspberry jam.

7. Place the disc in the bottom of the mould and spoon in the filling. Chill, then remove from the mould.

* This cake should be eaten very cold, soon after it is made.
* I suggest that you serve the cheese cake with fresh raspberries and a coulis of raspberries – fresh raspberries crushed with sugar.
* You can glaze the cheese cake by dusting it with caster sugar and passing a little red-hot salamander over the surface.

Gâteau de crêpes "Nicole Seitz"
Pancakes "Nicole Seitz"

Preparation time: 1¼ hours
Oven temperature: 350°F/180°C/Gas 4

For eight people

For the Pancakes
250 g (8¾ oz) flour
75 g (2½ oz) sugar
5 eggs
a pinch of salt
150 g (¼ pint) double cream
50 g (2 oz) butter
500 ml (scant pint) milk
1½ tablespoons Grand Marnier

For the Soufflé
12 egg yolks
6 tablespoons sugar
6 egg whites
zest of an orange
1½ tablespoons Grand Marnier
a little icing sugar

"Nicole Seitz est une merveilleuse ambassadrice des cuisiniers et de la cuisine française. Nous lui devons beaucoup pour sa générosité à l'occasion des concours de cuisine et pour beaucoup d'autres choses, entre autres sa célèbre sympathie."

MAKING THE PANCAKES

1. Work the flour, sugar and eggs together in a bowl, then mix in the salt and cream. Add the butter, melted, and gradually dilute with the milk and Grand Marnier. If the batter seems lumpy strain it through a fine strainer.

2. Butter a heavy pan and make 10-12 pancakes.

3. Butter the inside of a genoise mould and sprinkle with sugar. Line the sides and bottom of the tin with the pancakes, keeping two or three back to cover the top.

MAKING THE SOUFFLE

4. Preheat the oven. Whisk the egg yolks with 3 tablespoons of sugar until pale. Beat the egg whites to a snow, adding the remaining 3 tablespoons of sugar. Fold the egg yolks and whites together and incorporate the orange zest and Grand Marnier carefully, using a palette knife. Pour into the mould lined with pancakes and cover loosely with the remaining pancakes.

5. Cook in the oven for 20 minutes.

6. Serve as soon as the soufflé has cooked, sprinkled with icing sugar.

* This dessert must be eaten as soon as it has cooked, because it is, simply, a soufflé encased in pancakes.

Russe au chocolat
Chocolate Russe

Preparation time: 40 minutes plus cooling time
Oven temperature: 350°F/180°C/Gas 4

For six people

For the Base
7 egg whites
80 g (3¼ oz) ground almonds
80 g (3¼ oz) icing sugar
60 g (2 oz) granulated sugar
15 g (½ oz) unsweetened cocoa powder

For the Chocolate Mousse
250 ml (scant half pint) milk
4 egg yolks
100 g (3½ oz) sugar
125 g (4½ oz) dark cooking chocolate
350 ml (⅔ pint) whipping cream
3 leaves of gelatine

MAKING THE MERINGUES

1. Preheat the oven. Mix the almonds, icing sugar, cocoa and 2 of the egg whites together in a bowl. Whisk the remaining 5 egg whites to a snow, add the granulated sugar and fold the egg whites carefully into the cocoa mixture. Butter a sheet of baking paper and pipe onto it 12 rounds of the biscuit mixture 4″ across. Sprinkle with icing sugar and bake in the oven, with the door ajar, for 20-25 minutes.

MAKING THE CHOCOLATE MOUSSES

2. Bring the milk to the boil. Meanwhile beat the egg yolks and the sugar to a foam in a bowl. Pour in the hot milk, whisking all the time and return to the saucepan. Bring the mixture up to 185°F/85°C and keep it there for 3 minutes or until the mixture coats the back of a spoon.

3. Soften the gelatine in cold water for 10 minutes. Cut the dark chocolate into chunks and pour the hot custard over it. Mix until the chocolate has all melted. Squeeze the gelatine and mix in to the chocolate custard. Whip the cream and when the custard is cold, fold it in.

4. Place one meringue on each plate, spread it with ½″ layer of chocolate mousse, and top with a second meringue.

* This dessert can be served accompanied by a chilled chocolate sauce.

Gâteau Russe au praliné
Praline Gâteau

Preparation time: 45 minutes
Oven temperature: 475°F/250°C/Gas 9

For six   *For the Base*
people   70 g (2½ oz) sugar
70 g (2½ oz) ground almonds
5 egg whites

For the Praline Mousse
200 g (7 oz) butter
200 g (7 oz) powdered praline
3 egg whites
300 g (10½ oz) sugar

MAKING THE BASE
1. Preheat the oven to its hottest setting. Mix the sugar, almonds and one of the egg whites in a bowl. Whisk the other 4 egg whites to a snow and mix carefully with the sugar and almonds. Butter a sheet of baking paper and spread out the mixture in a layer ¼" deep. Sprinkle with fine sugar and cook in the hot oven, door slightly ajar, for 8 minutes. Remove from the oven before the base becomes too crisp: it should be eaten soft.

MAKING THE PRALINE MOUSSE
2. Whisk the butter and the praline together in a bowl. Cook the sugar with a little water until it reaches 250°F/120°C, hard ball stage, and meanwhile beat the egg whites to a snow. Pour the hot sugar on to the egg whites in a stream, whisking, and continue beating until the mixture is cold.

3. Mix the praline and butter mixture and the "Italian" meringue together carefully.

ASSEMBLING THE GATEAU
4. Cut two equal rectangles out of the base (1). Spread three quarters of the mousse on one of them, smoothing the top with a palette knife, and cover with the second rectangle. Pipe the remaining mousse over the top in an attractive pattern with a medium piping bag fitted with a star nozzle.

* Care is needed when cooking the base. It tends to dry out as it cools and should therefore be taken out of the oven when it is still moist and soft.

"Un gâteau au praliné pas très sucré dont la réussite dépend de la finesse du biscuit."

Macaronade au citron
Lemon Macaroons

Preparation time: 45 minutes
Oven temperature: 400°F/200°C/Gas 6

For ten
people

For the Macaroon
250 g (8¾ oz) icing sugar
100 g (3½ oz) ground almonds
4 egg whites
grated zest of 2 lemons

For the Lemon Mousse
5 leaves of gelatine
500 ml (scant pint) whipping cream
400 ml (scant ¾ pint) lemon juice
200 g (7 oz) sugar

"Une pâte de macaron garnie d'une mousse légère, un mélange subtil."

MAKING THE MACAROONS

1. Preheat the oven. Sieve 200 g (7 oz) of the icing sugar and the powdered almonds together.

2. Whisk the egg whites to a snow with the remaining 50 g (1¾ oz) icing sugar. Fold in the sieved sugar and almonds and the lemon zest.

3. Pipe the mixture on to a sheet of baking paper with a piping bag with a ¼″ nozzle to form 20 discs 4″ in diameter. Bake for 15 minutes, with the oven door barely ajar to avoid the build-up of steam.

MAKING THE LEMON MOUSSE

4. Soften the gelatine for ten minutes in cold water. Whip the cream and chill. Squeeze excess moisture out of the gelatine and dissolve it in a little lemon juice over a low heat. When it is completely dissolved add the rest of the lemon juice and cool over a bowl of ice.

5. Just as the lemon mixture is beginning to set, fold it into the whipped cream together with the sugar.

ASSEMBLING THE LEMON MACAROONS

6. Spread half the circles of macaroon with the mousse and top with the remaining circles. You will have ten little sandwiches of macaroon and lemon mousse.

* This dessert should be eaten cool but not iced. It can be served with a sweet purée of soft fruit.

Charlotte choco-poires
Chocolate and Pear Mousse

Preparation time: 1 hour
Oven temperature: 425°F/200°C/Gas 7

For six people

For the Base
3 eggs
120 g (4¼ oz) sugar
120 g (4¼ oz) flour, sifted

For the Chocolate Mousse
250 ml (scant half pint) milk
3 egg yolks
100 g (3½ oz) sugar
125 g (4¼ oz) dark chocolate, broken up
3 leaves of gelatine
300 ml (½ pint) whipping cream

For the Pear Mousse
250 g (9 oz) pears peeled, cored and puréed
50 g (1¾ oz) sugar
2 leaves of gelatine
300 ml (½ pint) whipping cream
½ pear, sliced
1 teaspoon lemon juice

MAKING THE BASE

1. Preheat the oven. Separate the egg whites from the yolks and whisk the whites with an electric beater until they are very stiff. Mix in the sugar. Beat the egg yolks with a fork and carefully fold in the sifted flour and the egg whites. Butter a sheet of baking paper and spread the mixture in a layer. Bake for 8-10 minutes. The base should remain soft.

MAKING THE CHOCOLATE MOUSSE

2. Beat the egg yolks and the sugar. Bring the milk to the boil and pour onto the yolks. Mix and return to the saucepan. Cook gently, without boiling, until the mixture coats the back of a spoon – about 3 minutes at 185°F/85°C.

3. Pour the custard on to the broken-up chocolate and stir until the chocolate is completely dissolved. Soften the gelatine in a little cold water for 10 minutes. Squeeze the water out of the gelatine and stir into the hot chocolate custard. Allow to become cold, then whip the cream and fold it in very carefully.

MAKING THE PEAR MOUSSE

4. Soften the gelatine in a little cold water for 10 minutes then dissolve it in a little of the pear purée with the sugar. Then heat it gently in a small pan, add the rest of the purée, and allow to get cold. Whip the cream and fold it in carefully.

FINISHING AND SERVING THE DISH

5. Line the bottom and sides of a charlotte mould with the base, using strips to line the sides. Fill half full with the chocolate mousse (3) and then fill to the brim with the pear mousse (4). Chill again and turn out on to a serving plate. Decorate the top with a few slices of pear dipped in lemon juice, in a rosette. Serve with a chocolate sauce sweetened to taste.

Soufflés chauds au chocolat
Hot Chocolate Soufflés

Preparation time: 15 minutes
Oven temperature: 425°F/220°C/Gas 7

For four people

a little butter
8 egg yolks
4 tablespoons sugar
4 tablespoons unsweetened cocoa powder
grated zest of 1 lemon
12 egg whites

1. Preheat the oven. Butter four individual soufflé dishes and sprinkle the insides with caster sugar.

2. Beat together the egg yolks, the sugar, the cocoa and the lemon zest. Whisk the egg whites with a small pinch of sugar and fold them into the egg yolks.

3. Fill each individual soufflé dish to the rim and cook in the oven for 12 minutes.

4. Serve the soufflés just as they are, straight from the oven.

* These soufflés must be eaten as soon as they are cooked. If they have to wait they will collapse.
* The same mixture can be used to make one big soufflé.

Gâteau de poires chaudes au beurre de cacao
Hot Pear Pastries with Chocolate Sauce

Preparation time: 45 minutes
Oven temperature: 475°F/240°C/Gas 9

For six people

6 ripe pears
500 g (18 oz) sugar
filo pastry
2 egg yolks
50 g (1¾ oz) unsweetened cocoa powder
50 g (1¾ oz) cocoa butter

1. Peel, halve and core the pears and poach them in a syrup made with the sugar dissolved in 1 litre (1¾ pints) water.

2. Preheat oven to its highest setting. When the pears have cooled, cut them into quarters and wrap each quarter in one or more sheets of filo pastry. Brush with beaten egg yolk.

3. Place the pear "parcels" on an oiled baking tray and cook for 8-9 minutes.

TO MAKE THE SAUCE
4. Mix the cocoa into 300 ml (½ pint) water and boil to reduce slightly. Whisk in the cocoa butter.

* This dessert should be eaten very hot and very crisp.
* Filo pastry can be bought in Greek shops and delicatessens. It is always delicious but can sometimes prove indigestible.

Editor's note Since filo pastry can be rather brittle and difficult to handle, it is sometimes helpful to brush the pastry with melted butter before folding it. If you find it difficult to cut with a knife, use scissors. Pack the pastries close together on the oiled baking tray, to prevent them unfolding as they cook.

ICED DESSERTS
AND ACCOMPANIMENTS

Soufflé glacé Créole
Iced Creole Soufflé

Preparation time: 1 hour, plus freezing time

For ten people

500 g (18 oz) plain bitter chocolate

For the chocolate mousse
5 egg yolks
200 g (7 oz) sugar
250 ml (scant half pint) milk
150 g (5¼ oz) unsweetened chocolate
500 ml (scant pint) liquid crème fraîche *or* whipping cream

For the pineapple mousse
250 g (8¾ oz) puréed pineapple
250 ml (scant ½ pint) liquid crème fraîche *or* whipping cream
3 egg whites
150 g (5¼ oz) sugar

1. Warm up 10 ramekins to 70°F/22°C approximately.

2. Melt the 500 g (18 oz) bitter chocolate in a bain-marie or double saucepan to 115°F/45°C. Pour it on to a clean marble slab and work it with a spatula until it begins to thicken at 68°-77°F/20–25°C. Return to the pan and heat to 88°F/31°C maximum, at which point the chocolate is "stabilised" and can be used to line the ramekins. Ladle a little chocolate into a ramekin, tilt it from side to side so that the whole of the interior is coated, pour off any surplus chocolate and place face-down on a sheet of greaseproof paper. Repeat with the other nine ramekins, and chill them for 2 hours in the refrigerator.

3. Ease each of the chocolate linings out of the ramekins, by pulling the edge gently. Keep them cold.

4. Beat the egg yolks with the sugar while you bring the milk to the boil. Pour the hot, but not quite boiling, milk on to the egg yolks, whisking, and mix well. Strain into the saucepan in which you have boiled the milk and heat for about 3 minutes at 185°F/85°C until the custard coats the back of the spoon. Away from the heat add the chocolate, in pieces, and stir until it has dissolved. Whip the 500 ml (scant pint) of cream while the chocolate-flavoured custard cools over ice, then fold them together carefully. Fill the chocolate moulds (3) three-quarters full and place them in the freezer. When they have frozen hard, give each mould a "collar" of greaseproof paper, tied in place with string, so that it sticks up 1-1½″ above the chocolate.

5. Whip the 250 ml (scant half pint) of cream and keep it cold. Heat the sugar in a little water to 250°F/121°C while you beat the egg whites to a stiff snow with an electric beater. Still beating, pour on the hot syrup and beat until cool. Fold half the whipped cream into the pineapple purée and the other half into the egg whites. Fold the two together very delicately.

6. Fill the moulds to the top of the collars with the pineapple mousse and freeze until firm. Remove the "collars" just before serving.

* Serve with a sweetened pineapple purée and decorate with slices of fresh pineapple.

Mousse à l'anis
Anise-flavoured Mousse

Preparation time: 30 minutes plus freezing time

For ten
people

8 egg yolks
20 g (¾ oz) star anise, crushed
150 g (5¼ oz) sugar
500 ml (scant pint) whipping cream
3 tablespoons pastis (Pernod or Ricard)

1. Beat the egg yolks vigorously with an electric beater until smooth and pale. Cook the sugar and the star anise with a little water to 250°F/121°C, hard ball stage. Strain the syrup on to the egg yolks, beating steadily until the mixture has cooled.

2. Whip the cream, incorporate the pastis and fold into the anise and egg mixture. Pour into a dish or soufflé mould and freeze immediately.

* This dessert should be eaten iced and accompanied by a purée of soft fruit such as strawberries, raspberries or loganberries.

"Un dessert plein de soleil pour faire suite à un dejeuner provençal."

Mousse au Whisky
Whisky Mousse

Preparation time: 20 minutes plus chilling time

For six people
250 ml (scant ½ pint) whipping cream
6 egg yolks
3 egg whites
100 g (3½ oz) sugar
6 tablespoons whisky

1. Prepare six individual soufflé dishes, giving each a "collar" of greaseproof paper secured with a rubber band or string.

2. Whisk the cream and chill it in the refrigerator.

3. Whisk the egg yolks with half the sugar, and then whisk the whites to a firm snow, with the remaining sugar. When the whites are holding their shape on the whisk, fold all the ingredients together carefully and mix in the whisky.

4. Fill the soufflé dishes with this mixture straight away, and put in the freezer.

5. Before serving, remove the paper "collars" and sprinkle the tops with icing sugar. The mousses should be served frozen.

* Whisky is one of the rare spirits which keeps its flavour when frozen.

Parfait glacé, sauce café grillé
Iced Coffee Parfait with Coffee Bean Sauce

Preparation time: 40 minutes plus chilling time

For ten people

For the Chocolate Mousse
5 egg yolks
200 g (7 oz) sugar
150 g (5¼ oz) unsweetened chocolate, broken into small pieces
250 ml (scant half pint) milk
500 ml (scant pint) whipping cream

For the Coffee Parfait
4 egg yolks
250 ml (scant half pint) whipping cream
a few drops of coffee flavouring
75 g (2½ oz) sugar

For the Sauce
500 ml (scant pint) milk
6 egg yolks
150 g (5¼ oz) sugar
50 g (1¾ oz) coffee beans

MAKING THE CHOCOLATE MOUSSE

1. Beat the egg yolks and the sugar together. Bring the milk to the boil and pour onto the egg yolks, mixing well. Return to the saucepan and cook over a gentle heat until the mixture coats the back of a spoon, bring up to 185°F/85°C and keep this temperature for 3 minutes, stirring. Remove from the heat and stir in the pieces of chocolate. When it has melted completely cool over cracked ice, stirring. Whip the cream, and fold it carefully into the mousse. Put out 10 individual soufflé dishes or ramekins and fill them one third full of mousse. Chill the ramekins in the refrigerator, but keep the remainder of the mousse at warm room temperature to prevent it setting.

MAKING THE COFFEE PARFAIT

2. Whip the cream until it is firm, flavour with the coffee essence and keep cold.

3. Cook the sugar with a little water until it reaches 250°F/121°C, hard ball stage, and meanwhile beat the egg yolks with an electric beater in a bowl, until they are thick and frothy. Pour the hot sugar syrup onto the yolks and beat with the electric beater until the mixture is quite cold. Then carefully fold in the whipped cream. Pour this parfait into the soufflé dishes, filling them to the two-thirds level, chill and finish by filling with the remaining chocolate mousse. Place the ramekins in the freezer.

MAKING THE ROASTED COFFEE SAUCE

4. Bring the milk to the boil. Whisk the 6 egg yolks with the sugar, pour on the milk and cook, stirring continuously, without boiling until the mixture coats the back of a spoon (as you did with the chocolate mousse custard in step 1).

5. Roast the coffee beans in a medium oven. Crush them and mix into the hot custard (4). Allow to cool and then chill.

6. Turn out the mousses on to ten small plates and pour the sauce round each one.

Poires farcis a la glace chicorée
Pears with Chicory Ice Cream

Preparation time: 45 minutes plus freezing time
Oven temperature: 400°F/200°C/Gas 6

For six
people

For the Pears
3 ripe pears
500 g (18 oz) sugar
juice of 1 lemon
1 vanilla pod
6½ tablespoons kirsch
1 teaspoon butter

For the Chicory Ice Cream
500 ml (scant pint) milk
100 ml (3½ oz) double cream
6 egg yolks
150 g (5¼ oz) sugar
a few drops of chicory extract

1. Peel the pears, dividing them into two, and core them neatly. Boil 500 g (18 oz) sugar in the same weight of water to make a light syrup, add the lemon juice and poach the pears. Let them cool in the syrup.

2. Bring the milk and cream to the boil together. Whisk the egg yolks and the sugar together in a bowl. Pour over the hot milk and mix well. Return to the saucepan in which you have boiled the milk and heat gently until the mixture will coat the back of a spoon. Add the chicory essence and freeze in electric ice cream maker or in trays in the freezer.

3. Preheat the oven. Arrange the halved pears in an enamelled iron casserole and pour over them 200 ml (⅓ pint) of the cooking syrup (1), add the kirsch and the vanilla pod. Cook in the oven for ten minutes.

4. Drain the pears reserving the syrup and place one half pear on each plate.

5. Boil the syrup rapidly with a nut of butter. Place a rounded spoonful of ice cream in the hollow of each half pear, and strain the sauce over the top. Serve immediately.

* This dessert must be assembled at the last moment, although the ice cream and the poached pears can be made ready in advance. Different flavours of ice cream can be tried.

Terrine de fruits marinés
Terrine of Marinated Fruits

Preparation time: 24 hours marination, 2 hours preparation plus freezing time

For ten people
250 g (8¾ oz) each of strawberries, pears, peaches, stoned prunes
2 litres (3½ pints) red Bordeaux wine
zests of 4 oranges
4 cinnamon sticks
400 g (14 oz) brown sugar
1 litre (1¾ pints) whipping cream
12 egg whites
600 g (1 lb 5 oz) caster sugar

"Tout le monde connaît les fruits en compote, pruneaux au vin, etc. J'ai réuni un ensemble de fruits macérés et les ai transformés en mousse."

1. Poach each fruit separately in a marinade made of 500 ml (scant pint) of wine, the zest of an orange, a cinnamon stick and 100 g (3½ oz) sugar, and leave to marinate, separately, for 24 hours.

ON THE DAY
2. Drain the fruits and purée them separately. Chill.

3. Whip the cream and chill.

4. Make four separate mousses out of the four fruits. For each, use a quarter of the whipped cream from the refrigerator, 3 egg whites and 150 g (5¼ oz) caster sugar, repeating the following procedures four times: Cook the sugar in a little water till it reaches 250°F/120°C, hard ball stage, and meanwhile whisk the egg whites to a snow. Pour the hot sugar in a stream on to the egg whites whisking all the time and continue to beat as it cools, to form an "Italian" meringue. Mix half the fruit purée with the meringue and half with the whipped cream and then fold one into the other with a spatula.

5. Have ready a rectangular terrine and, as you complete each mousse, pour it in and then put in the freezer to set before you make the next layer.

* This dessert should be served iced, in neat slices.
* It can be served with whole marinated fruits and a spoonful or two of the marinade.

Terrine aux chocolat et aux fruits
Chocolate Terrine

Preparation time: 50 minutes, plus freezing time

For five people

250 ml (scant half pint) milk
4 egg yolks
50 g (1¾ oz) sugar
5 leaves gelatine
40 g (1½ oz) dark sweetened chocolate, grated
25 g (1 oz) praline powder
40 g (1½ oz) dark bitter chocolate, grated
40 g (1½ oz) icing sugar
15 g (½ oz) grated fresh coconut
125 g (4½ oz) mashed banana
1 leaf gelatine
500 ml (scant pint) liquid crème fraîche *or* whipping cream

1. Put the milk to heat in a pan and bring to the boil; meanwhile beat the egg yolks with the sugar in a bowl until they turn a pale creamy colour. Pour the hot but not quite boiling milk over the yolks, whisking, and return the mixture to the pan. Cook for about 3 minutes over a low heat, 185°F/85°C or until the mixture coats the back of a spoon. Strain into a bowl.

2. Meanwhile, soak the 5 leaves of gelatine in a little cold water. Squeeze them and combine with the hot custard (1), stirring until completely melted.

3. Divide the custard between three bowls. Into the first, stir the sweetened chocolate with the praline; and into the second stir the bitter chocolate and the icing sugar, whisking vigorously to obtain a smooth mixture. Mix the grated coconut into the third bowl.

4. Soak the single leaf of gelatine in cold water, and melt it in a small pan. Add it to the banana pulp in a fourth bowl and mix well.

5. Whip the cream with a balloon whisk and divide it equally between the four bowls. Fold it in very delicately.

6. Assemble the terrine in a china dish, spooning in a layer of bitter chocolate, a layer of coconut, a layer of praline and a layer of banana, and so on until the dish is full. Freeze, turn out on to a serving dish and slice while still firm.

* This dessert is eaten cold, with a fresh apricot or banana purée.

Candi de chicorée
Iced Chicory Mousse

Preparation time: 2 hours plus freezing time
Oven temperature: 400°F/200°C/Gas 6

For ten
people

2 eggs
60 g (2½ oz) sugar
60 g (2½ oz) sifted flour
500 ml (scant pint) milk
½ packet chicory (coffee substitute)
250 ml (scant ½ pint) whipping cream
3 egg whites
300 g (10½ oz) sugar

1. Preheat the oven. Whip the eggs and sugar in the top of a double boiler until they reach a temperature of 100°F/40°C. Remove from the heat and continue beating until the mixture is cold. Then beat in the sifted flour.

2. Spread the mixture on a sheet of baking paper on a baking sheet and bake in the oven without allowing steam to build up (leave the door very slightly ajar). Line the bottom of a small cake tin with this cooked sponge base, cutting it to fit.

3. Bring the milk and the chicory to the boil together. Allow the chicory to infuse for several minutes, then strain the flavoured milk through a very fine sieve into a bowl and chill. Whip the cream and chill it.

4. Cook the sugar with a little water until it reaches 250°F/121°C, hard ball stage. Meanwhile whip the egg whites to a snow and pour the hot sugar on to them, whisking all the time, to make an Italian meringue.

5. Mix half the chilled flavoured milk with the cooled meringue and half with the chilled whipped cream. Fold these two mixtures together and pour into the cake tin. Put in the freezer to stiffen. Turn out of the tin to serve.

* This dessert is eaten iced, accompanied by a rich custard lightly flavoured with chicory and sweetened to taste.

"Des souvenirs de café à la chicorée m'ont amené à créer ce dessert plein d'odeur avec une pointe d'amertume très agréable."

Soupe de clementines
Clementines with their Sorbet

Preparation time: 1 hour plus freezing time

For six people

25 clementines
200 g (7 oz) sugar
50 g (1¾ oz) honey
100 g (3½ oz) butter
6 sprigs of mint

PRELIMINARY PREPARATIONS

1. Peel 15 of the clementines, removing all the pith, and skin the segments. Arrange them in rosettes on six plates.

2. Squeeze the remaining 10 clementines to produce 500 ml (scant pint) juice. Add the sugar, and pour into an electric ice cream maker, keeping back a couple of tablespoons to make the sauce. When the sorbet is ready, store it in the freezer.

MAKING THE HONEY SAUCE

3. Caramelise the honey over a low heat in a heavy pan and moisten with a little clementine juice. Bring to the boil, add the butter cut into cubes and whisk with an electric beater until the mixture is smooth.

FINISHING AND SERVING THE DISH

4. Put a scoop of clementine sorbet (2) in the middle of each rosette of clementine segments and pour over a little of the honey sauce. Decorate with a sprig of mint and serve immediately.

* Oranges and grapefruit can be used to give an equally successful result.

"A la fois rafraîchissant et tiède, une façon d'utiliser en pleine période de production les magnifiques fruits de Corse ou d'Eze."

Entremets glace sabayon au porto
Port Zabaglione Ice Cream

Preparation time: 45 minutes plus freezing time

For ten people

For the Zabaglione
8 egg yolks
250 ml (scant half pint) port
250 g (9 oz) sugar
500 ml (scant pint) whipping cream

For the Sauce
2 ripe melons
100 g (3½ oz) sugar

1. Bring the port and the sugar to the boil and meanwhile whisk the egg yolks with an electric beater until smooth and pale. Pour the hot syrup onto the egg yolks and beat gently until the mixture is completely cold. Whip the cream and fold it into the egg mixture.

2. Have ready eight small circular moulds 4-4½″ in diameter (or 8 circles made of stiff card stapled together) on a tray covered with baking paper. Fill with the mixture and freeze immediately.

3. For the sauce, purée the flesh of the melons with 100 g (3½ oz) sugar. Serve this sauce very cold in a bowl or sauce boat.

* This frozen sabayon has an astonishing lightness. We discovered it when we had frozen some zabaglione after making too much. We had a pleasant surprise when we tasted it later.

Glace aux pointes d'asperges
Asparagus Ice Cream

Preparation time: 25 minutes plus 36 hours

For six to eight people

500 g (18 oz) asparagus
200 g (7 oz) double cream *or* crème fraîche
750 ml (1¼ pints) milk
12 egg yolks
300 g (10½ oz) sugar

MAKING THE ASPARAGUS ICE CREAM

1. Cook the asparagus in unsalted water until tender, then purée it. Sieve the purée to remove any fibres. Meanwhile, bring the cream and the milk to the boil together.

2. Beat the egg yolks with the sugar and pour on the hot milk and cream. Stir and return to the saucepan, cooking over a gentle heat until the mixture coats the back of a spoon – about 3 minutes at 180°F/85°C. Fold the custard into the asparagus purée, and put to freeze in an electric ice cream maker.

* If you have time, you can decorate the ice with crystallised asparagus tips made by boiling 1 kg (2¼ lbs) sugar with 500 ml (scant pint) water, adding the asparagus tips and, after boiling briefly, allowing them to cool and macerate in the syrup for 36 hours.

* Serve in individual bowls or in a large frosted bowl.

Glace à l'essence de pin
Pine Ice Cream

Preparation time: 20 minutes plus freezing time

For six to eight people

1 litre (1¾ pints) milk
200 ml (⅓ pint) double cream *or* crème fraîche
12 egg yolks
250 g (8¾ oz) sugar
a few drops essential oil of pine (from a herbalist)

Bring the milk and the cream to the boil together. Beat the egg yolks and sugar together in a bowl, and pour on the boiling milk. Stir and return to the saucepan. Cook over a gentle heat without boiling at 185°F/85°C until the mixture coats the back of a spoon – about 3 minutes. Cool over a bowl of ice and when it is cold mix in the pine oil. Sieve and freeze in an electric ice cream maker. Do not waste time at this stage, as the precious aroma of the pine will evaporate. Serve in individual ice cream dishes or as part of an arrangement of assorted desserts.

Glace aux kumquats et Grand Marnier
Kumquat Ice Cream with Grand Marnier

Preparation time: 20 minutes plus freezing time

For six to eight people

400 g (14 oz) kumquats
750 ml (1¼ pints) milk
200 ml (⅓ pint) double cream *or* crème fraîche
12 egg yolks
300 g (10½ oz) sugar
50 g (1¾ oz) Grand Marnier

Cut the kumquats in half, remove the seeds and purée them, skins and all. Sieve the purée. Bring the milk and cream to the boil while you beat the egg yolks and sugar in a bowl. Pour over the boiling milk, stir and return to the saucepan. Cook over a gentle heat without boiling until the mixture coats the back of a spoon – for about 3 minutes at 185°F/85°C. Mix this custard with the kumquat purée and when it has cooled, add the Grand Marnier. Freeze in an electric ice cream maker.

Serve three scoops of ice cream to each person, topped with a hollowed-out kumquat filled with a spoonful of ice cream.

* This delicious little citrus fruit is eaten candied, preserved in alcohol, and sometimes raw with sugar.

Sorbet Suze
Suze Sorbet

Preparation time: 15 minutes plus freezing time

For six to eight people
400 g (14 oz) sugar
200 ml (⅓ pint) Suze
juice of 1 lemon

Boil the sugar with 800 ml (scant 1½ pints) water for five minutes to make the syrup. Allow to cool and mix in the Suze and lemon juice. Freeze immediately in an electric ice cream maker.

Serve in individual bowls or in a big chilled bowl.

* This rather bitter sorbet can be served between courses as a kind of "trou normand" or it makes a good "digestif" finish to a meal.

Sorbet romarin
Rosemary Sorbet

Preparation time: 15 minutes plus freezing time

For six to
ght people
350 g (12½ oz) sugar
30 g (1 oz) fresh rosemary spikes
juice of 1 lemon
1 litre (1¾ pints) water
a few sprigs of fresh mint

Boil the sugar, rosemary and lemon juice with the water and allow to infuse for 15 minutes. Strain through a cloth or fine sieve and freeze immediately in an electric ice cream maker. Serve each person with three scoops of sorbet, topped with a small sprig of mint.

* Like the Suze sorbet, this sorbet can be served as a 'trou normand' or eaten as a truly delicious *digestif* dessert.

Sorbet cacao-menthe
Chocolate-Mint Sorbet

Preparation time: 15 minutes plus freezing time

For six to   300 g (10½ oz) sugar
eight   100 g (3½ oz) cocoa
people   5 tablespoons colourless mint liqueur

Boil the sugar with 300 ml (½ pint) water for 5 minutes to make the syrup. Mix in the cocoa. Allow to cool and add the mint liqueur and 500 ml (scant pint) water. Freeze in an electric ice cream maker. Serve three scoops of sorbet to each person or serve in a frosted bowl.

* This sorbet can be served with a light chocolate sauce made of milk, sugar and cocoa – the proportions can be varied according to your taste.

Gaufres de Palmyre
Palmyre's Waffles

Preparation time: 20 minutes plus 1 hour chilling

For approximately 50 waffles

5 egg yolks
250 ml (scant half pint) milk
1 tablespoon sugar, or more to taste
1 pinch salt
500 g (18 oz) softened butter
275 g (10 oz) flour

1. Mix the egg yolks, milk, sugar and salt together thoroughly in a large bowl.

2. Fold in the flour, working it gently until you have a dough similar to a light pâte sablée. The exact quantity of flour will depend on the type used. Add the softened butter and mix again.

3. Wrap the dough in plastic film and let it rest in a cool place for 1 hour. Then, roll out to a thickness of ¼″.

4. Cut the pastry into small circles with a round cutter and cook them on both sides in a waffle iron or on a heated griddle. Sprinkle them with caster sugar and serve warm.

Tuiles aux pignons et à l'essence de pin
Pine-nut Tuiles

Preparation time: 20 minutes
Oven temperature: 425°F/220°C/Gas 7

For approximately 50 tuiles

6 egg whites
200 g (7 oz) sugar
250 g (8¾ oz) pine-nuts
125 g (4½ oz) flour
125 g (4½ oz) melted butter
5 drops of pine essence

1. Preheat the oven. Mix the egg whites and sugar together with a whisk. Incorporate the pine-nuts and then the flour with a wooden spoon. Whisk the flour with a spatula, and when they are thoroughly incorporated, fold in the melted butter and the pine essence.

2. Butter a baking sheet and spoon little mounds of the mixture evenly over it. Flatten each little mound with a moistened fork.

3. Bake in the hot oven for approximately 10 minutes. As soon as the tuiles are cooked, remove them with a spatula from the baking sheet and "shape" them while they are still hot and flexible by placing them on suitably shaped round objects – rolling-pins or small bottles, for example. If they are not to be eaten immediately, the tuiles should be stored in a dry place.

Pâte de fruits rouge
Red Fruit Comfits

Preparation time: 15 minutes, plus two hours chilling time

For four people
250 g (8¾ oz) liquidised or sieved uncooked soft fruit such as strawberries, raspberries, currants, blackcurrants
250 g (8¾ oz) sugar
25 g (1 oz) fruit pectin

1. Mix the sugar with the pectin, and add half this mixture to the fruit in an enamelled or stainless-steel pan. Bring to the boil, add the rest of the sugar and pectin, return to the boil and cook briskly for 4 minutes.

2. Pour the fruit into a shallow metal tray, and let it cool for 2 hours. Cut into squares with a sharp knife and roll each comfit in sugar.

* By cooking the fruit very rapidly, the flavour, nutritional value, colour and aroma are all preserved.

Sablés au chocolat
Little Chocolate Biscuits

Preparation time: 1½ hours
Oven temperature: 450°F/230°C/Gas 8

For approximately 50 biscuits

180 g (6½ oz) butter
150 g (5¼ oz) caster sugar
1 egg
3 tablespoons milk
300 g (10½ oz) flour
30 g (1 oz) cornflour
1 teaspoon baking powder
dark plain chocolate

1. Cream the butter with the sugar until it is smooth, then add the egg and the milk and mix again. Fold in the dry ingredients carefully. Refrigerate the dough for 20 minutes. Preheat the oven.

2. Pipe the dough onto a buttered baking sheet in whatever shapes you fancy. Leave the baking sheet in the refrigerator to set for 15 minutes and then bake in the hot oven for 10 minutes.

3. Dip the cooled biscuits, partly or completely, into melted chocolate. If they are not to be eaten immediately, store in a dry cool place.

Truffes au Curaçao
Curaçao Truffles

Preparation time: 30 minutes

For approximately 100 truffles

8 tablespoons liquid crème fraîche *or* whipping cream
20 g (⅔ oz) butter
250 g (8¾ oz) plain dark chocolate
3 tablespoons Curaçao

For the icing
250 g (8¾ oz) plain dark chocolate
100 g (3½ oz) unsweetened cocoa powder

1. Cut 250 g (8¾ oz) of chocolate into small pieces and put them in a bowl. Bring the cream and butter to the boil and pour over the chocolate. Whisk till smooth and allow to cool.

2. Mix in the Curaçao and pipe the mixture in small balls onto a sheet of greaseproof paper. Chill.

3. Melt the remaining chocolate in a small pan. Remove the truffles from the paper and shape them evenly by rolling them, one by one, between the palms of your hands. Dip each one in the melted chocolate and roll in the cocoa. If they are not to be eaten immediately the truffles should be stored in a dry cool place.

Nougats aux pistaches
Pistachio Nougat

Preparation time: 2 hours

For
approxi-
mately 50
small
pieces of
nougat

200 g (7 oz) sugar
40 g (1½ oz) glucose
1 large or 2 small egg whites
120 g (4¼ oz) honey
200 g (7 oz) toasted blanched almonds
60 g (2 oz) pistachios, skinned
60 g (2 oz) chopped crystallised fruit

1. Heat the sugar and glucose with 6 tablespoons water to 291°F/144°C, and meanwhile beat the egg whites to a stiff snow with an electric beater. Heat the honey to 250°F/121°C. Pour the hot syrup over the egg whites, keeping the beater running, and finally beat in the heated honey.

2. Stop the beater and transfer the mixture into a saucepan standing in a bain-marie over a low heat. Stir continually until the nougat has dried out and thickened. This is quite a long process, taking from 30 minutes to 1 hour.

3. When the nougat comes away easily from the sides of the pan, add the nuts and fruit and mix well. Spread the nougat out, on greaseproof paper, using a rolling-pin. Allow to dry for several hours and then cut into squares.

* You can give your nougat a personal touch by dipping the underside of each square in melted chocolate.

CONVERSION
AND TEMPERATURE TABLES

Conversion Tables

WEIGHT

1. Exact equivalents (to two places of decimals)

Metric	British
25 g	0.88 oz
100 g	3.53 oz
1 kg	2.20 lb

British	Metric
1 oz	28.35 g
8 oz	226.78 g
1 lb	0.45 kg (453.6 g)
1½ lb	0.68 kg (680.40 g)
2 lb	0.91 kg (907.2 g)

2. Approximate equivalents

Metric	British
25 g	1 oz
50 g	1¾-2 oz
75 g	2½ oz
100 g	3½ oz
200 g	7 oz
500 g (0.5 kg)	1 lb 2 oz (18 oz)
1000 g (1 kg)	2¼ lb (36 oz)

LIQUID MEASURES

1. Exact equivalents (to two places of decimals)

Metric	*British*
250 ml (0.25 litre)	0.44 pints
500 ml (0.50 litre)	0.88 pints
1 litre	1.76 pints

British	*Metric*
½ pint	0.28 litres
1 pint	0.57 litres

2. Approximate equivalents

Metric	*British*
150 ml	¼ pint
250 ml	scant half pint
300 ml	½ pint
500 ml (0.5 litre)	scant pint
750 ml	1¼ pints
1000 ml (1 litre)	1¾ pints
1.5 litres	2½ pints
2 litres	3½ pints

OVEN TEMPERATURES

Temperature equivalents for oven thermostat markings

Degrees Fahrenheit (°F)	Gas Regulo Mark	Degrees Centigrade (°C)
225	¼	110
250	½	130
275	1	140
300	2	150
325	3	170
350	4	180
375	5	190
400	6	200
425	7	220
450	8	230
475	9	240
500	10	250

Sugar Temperatures

Many of the recipes in this book require sugar to be heated with water to a specified temperature. For this you should ideally have a special sugar thermometer, preferably with a clip which fits over the edge of the pan. If you have no thermometer, the tests described in the following table should be carried out.

Sugar should be as far as possible dissolved in the water before boiling, and should not be stirred while boiling unless the recipe specifically instructs you to do so. Remove the pan from the heat immediately the desired temperature has been reached.

The "Italian meringue" which Jacques Maximin uses in many of his recipes calls for sugar heated to 250°F/121°C.

°F	°C	Description	Test
215-220	100-105	"Smooth"	Liquid becomes syrupy.
235-245	113-118	"Soft Ball"	A drop of syrup forms a soft ball when put in cold water.
245-265	118-130	"Hard Ball"	A drop of syrup forms a firm but malleable ball in cold water.
270-290	132-143	"Soft Crack"	A drop of syrup separates in cold water into separate but soft threads.
300–310	150–155	"Hard Crack"	A drop of syrup separates in cold water into brittle threads.
155	300	"Caramel"	The syrup becomes golden-brown.

INDEX

Index